"Heloise" and ot

David Abbey

2014

Index

HELOISE

A Monologue

HELOISE

Heloise, in her early 60's, is the Abbess of a French Benedictine convent. Though quite old by the standards of the early 12th century she is strong physically and at times projects a deep sensuality which contrasts with her position and our expectations.

THE SETTING

The action takes place in a crypt or nave within a convent (the Paraclette). The only props are a small bouquet of flowers, a sheaf of manuscript pages and a casket which is probably best set on a low riser.

(At rise the coffin is seen. On it is a small bouquet of flowers.)

(HEOISE, carrying a sheaf of manuscript pages, approaches the casket, regards it quietly.)

HELOISE ADDRESSES THE COFFIN

PATER NOSTER, qui es in caelis, sanctificetur nomen tuum. Adveniat regnum tuum. Fiat voluntas tua, sicut in caelo et in terra. Panem nostrum quotidianum da nobis hodie, et dimitte nobis debita nostra sicut et nos dimittimus debitoribus nostris. Et ne nos inducas in tentationem, sed libera nos a malo. Amen.

(She stands looking bewildered.)

The sisters sing mass,
To honour this day.
Our spiritual father has returned.

Your corpse now completes its journey
Arriving here by my invitation.

But I did not ask for *this!*

(SLAMS the papers onto the coffin)

This is not addressed to me!
Yet, within its covers
Is my name.
Indeed it has within it
My life.
Our life.
The front is emblazoned as
"The Story of My Misfortune";
You say, within, that it is written,
"To a friend"
So that he might feel less pain
By contrasting his ills
With yours.

How could this be?
How have I become
Caught up in the sharing
Of a story which
By rights, is mine, is me.
Now, in God"s house,
You will hear of our life, from me.

TO THE AUDIENCE

I am Heloise.
In one thousand ninety-five, in Rouen,
A village by the Seine

One hundred twenty miles from Paris
My life began.
My mother had a noble bearing

And friends and lovers among nobility.
About my father there is some uncertainty
Say kindly, that he provided *in absentia*.

I was, I am told, an impossibly curious child.
Speech came early, as did the gift of mimicry;
What I could not understand I faithfully repeated
Sounding like my elders
In whichever tongue they used.

So, gradually, with court and Church and school
I gained the languages of Socrates and Samuel

I spent, some said
Too much of life with books
But did not feel the least deprived
For time and space were quite at hand.

There were always adults and their brood
Milling 'bout the dining room and
Oft' times mother took me to recitals
Escorted by my Uncle Fulbert.

Uncle - later Canon – Fulbert,
A kindly soul, given to drink in the evening
Quite doting on my mother,
Would visit unannounced
But seemed welcomed nonetheless.

He would bring me small pastries and
The occasional chemise from Paris
And would coax me into prancing
Across the moonlit patio
Or playing at rough-house games.

We would surely end up lying upon the floor
Or hanging one upon the other,
Convulsed with laughter.

At these times, he would hold me close, Stroke
my hair and pronounce me
The most beautiful, the most charming young girl
In all of France.

He teased my mother
That some day he would steal me away
And walk me on his arm
Along the streets of Paris
That the whole world could envy him.

In my 17th year, illness felled my mother and
To ease her burden
My uncle invited me to stay with him in Paris,
Promising my mother
He would provide for me,
Introduce me
And further my education In
every way possible.

And so I moved to Paris
Lived within the shadow of Notre Dame
And found my uncle was content
To lead me on his arm to Mass
And by nights
To have me read to him
Or provide the meaning
Or translation of some obscure reference.

I saw almost at once
That if I were the one to be further educated
Then the burden of finding a tutor would be mine.

At that time I heard,
While in the streets, or at market and
Even from our housekeeper,
Of Master Peter Abelard,
Given the title by almost everyone
As the greatest philosopher in the world,
Although some would limit the area to Europe,
And others just to France.

TO THE COFFIN

It was a ringing endorsement

By anyone who claimed to have heard you – Or even to
have met one of your students.

Not only was your scholarship praised
But everyone held you in high regard
Because of your devotion to your work
And to your students.
Apparently, you were no stranger to the bistros of Paris
Nor to the vineyards all about;

But you did not consort with *"les femmes de joie"*,
And all esteemed you for your celibacy.

That quality all the more remarkable
Because of your good looks and age. While
most young men of twenty

Had already tasted of the body's pleasures
It was said that you, at thirty-five,
Had yet to dine.

Without difficulty,
I was able to find the place where you taught
At one of the schools of Notre Dame.
Standing to one side of an open door
Feigning discussion with a flower seller, I was able
to hear the disputation

And then the silence as you deftly drew
A thesis to its razor-sharp, concluding edge.

After some hours, you left;
Surrounded by a horde of jabbering youth
But even then continued with your lecture;
Challenging, mocking, falling back in a swoon
At a point deftly made,
Only to come charging back with a rejoinder.

It seemed to me that every day
The crowd of students grew larger,
The noise of the class more raucous,
And your swagger
A little more arrogant.
In fact, I would say you swaggered
With the self importance
Of a cock among his flock.

HELOISE TO HERSELF

I could not imagine
What sort of man
Would lecture for hours and then,
Accompanied by most of his students,

Would repair to one of the nearby auberges
To mix wine with dialectics.
As the crowd reached the establishment,
And almost as though a bell had been rung
To summon them,

A gaggle of women of all ages and descriptions –
Responding to the signal -
Would converge from surrounding streets and lanes
Inserting themselves into the throng.

I must confess
That on the one hand I was disgusted;
While on the other hand,
I was suddenly excited by the fantasy
Of joining all those young people,
And in particular sharing with them
All manner of songs and ribaldry.

TO THE COFFIN

I learned that many of the songs
Sung throughout the city
Were penned by you

And that many a young woman
Found herself described

Or her virtues extolled
Within the lyrics.
However, the dark side of such gatherings
The lechery and licentiousness
Both for me unknown,

Terrified me as much as it excited me
And I worked to suppress my images.

In time, you recognized me,
And sometimes smiled in my direction.
I was excited, embarrassed and confused;
Afraid you would say something to me, hoping you might.

One evening, my uncle Fulbert
Preparing for his canonical duties
Remarked he needed the skills of an Abelard
To solve the mystery of a certain piece of scripture.
Then, without pause,
He announced he would pose the question to you directly
And, if I had no objection,
Would invite you to dine with us.

HELOISE TO HERSELF

My momentary terror was quick eclipsed
By an excitement and wild rush of breath.
I could conjure no valid reason for objection and
Despite my racing heart
Decided I could withstand a conversation
With a figure so illustrious and learned.

TO THE COFFIN

Indeed, having heard your lectures
I knew that should the evening pursuits
Veer towards controversial or obscure matters

I might be able to contribute something of interest;
Or at least something
Which was more than token acquiescence
To whatever was said by host or guest.

The dinner was set for a week hence,
My uncle having sent a message to you
Offering not only a fine meal but also,
As I later learned,
An opportunity to meet,
And I blush to repeat this,
"The most intellectually superior beauty In all of
France."

At that dinner,
You settled my uncle's quandary
In dazzling manner:

A quick reference to St. Jerome, A
quotation from Acquinas
And your own interpretation,
Dispensed with all confusion.

HELOISE TO HERSELF

The actual business of the evening thus concluded,
We had time for many pleasantries.
I sipped my wine
Played lady of the house;
Ordering clean bowls and platters
Dispatching the servant to fetch each course.

My uncle took great pains
To ask me wide-ranging questions
Of church and state, of tragedy and comedy
Of heroes and their wars.
In the end, I found myself quite exhausted

From the effort of recalling information
And translating from original sources

Which I did mainly for my uncle.
It became apparent you knew almost no Hebrew –
And I gained a certain advantage there –
When drawing upon the Sages
To defend a proposition
Concerning the ethics of a situation.

TO THE COFFIN

It appears you circled issues
Testing for weakness
Until, like a falcon,
You descended,
Driving your talons Into the argument
Then carrying off the prize.

HELOISE TO HERSELF

I grew weary and withdrew,

Stopping, hidden, outside the dining room,
To catch my breath and hear
Your manly form of chatter
Freed as it would be
From the constraint of female presence.

The conversation was disjointed.
My uncle extolled the virtues of his wine
About in the same proportion

As he did the glory of the Church
And my own character and fashion.

TO THE COFFIN

To my astonishment,
You made my uncle a proposition.
To help reduce your costs while teaching

You offered to live with my uncle and me,
Pay a modest rent and

At the same time act as my tutor
In the areas of philosophy, logic and,
To a lesser degree, physics and astronomy.

HELOISE TO HERSELF

All that in return for a small garret
In the eaves,

And the simple fare of a functionary
Within the church.

I knew nothing more than these facts,

Nothing more.
Yet my heart began to race.

TO THE COFFIN

My uncle, excited by the prospect
Of so illustrious a boarder
One who would not only pay

But also contribute towards my learning
Leap't from his chair,
To embrace you
Sending flasks and platters flying.
In an instant,
A sum was agreed upon and a date for moving set.

HELOISE TO HERSELF

Standing in that hall,
I felt as though a blazing iron
Had suddenly been thrust into my chest.
My heart hammered wildly,
I could not catch my breath.
Now, in recall, that moment
Continues to thrill and excite me
Continues to bring heat to my face and loins.
For until that moment
I had not entertained anything more
Than a fleeting thought
That Master Abelard might be someone
To know from afar;
Perhaps someone with whom I could pass a word or two
On a chance meeting in Church.

TO THE COFFIN

Now, in one bolt,
You were to be a lodger under our roof and
We were to be as master and student.

I could barely understand what I was hearing,
Certainly did not understand
My body's response to this development.

You continued for a few more moments,
My uncle advising that,
If the occasion demanded,
You should have full authority to beat me.

That is, if I failed to study,
Or failed to please
Then I was to be treated

With whatever force was required
"To bring me round"
To do what I was told, as I was told.

Aghast, I moved to return to the room,
Then realized the challenge was one
From which I could flee.
To learn from the great Abelard
And to do it so well
You would have neither cause nor inclination
To raise your hand or voice against me.

HELOISE TO HERSELF

Several days later,
You and your servant Marcuse,
Brought the last of your belongings and
With much pushing and panting,

Installed it all in a small room under the eaves.
The boxes of books, instruments of astronomy,
Rolls of parchment, and wax tablets for messages
Entered the house like an invading army.

When everything had been installed
I could hear Marcuse softly singing
A song in which I thought I heard my own name,
Though I could not be certain.

TO THE COFFIN

Do you remember our first lesson Begun
on an Autumn afternoon
As cold as it was grey and unsettled?
Wind hammered at the walls and
We were forced to wrap ourselves in great pieces of fur.

I was keen to proceed but anxious.
I did not wish to disappoint
Nor run the risk of being punished.

"A Pretorian drives nails
Into the hands of Christ", you stated,
Then asked, "Did he sin?"
My mind raced and at once

I experienced your power as a teacher.
One who provokes with questions
While withholding hidden answers.
Indeed, how should I begin to answer?
Should I begin by defining sin?
Should I challenge your definition of the word?
Should I move deeper and ask whether the guard knew
His prisoner to be Christ?
Should I ask whether the man was simply obeying an order
And therefore the sin was not his but
That of his commander?

"You hesitate" you said.
"Because you have nothing to say,
Or because you have too much to say
And cannot order it in a meaningful way?"

"Neither", I replied. "I hesitate
Because we have not agreed upon the realm of discourse."
I asked you, "Are we to examine the motives for the act?
Are we to examine the act itself?
Or are we to examine,
The world in which the act took place ,
And the issues of responsibility for social order,
Which it is said directed that Christ be so treated?"

HELOISE TO HERSELF

I was astonished to hear myself.
My voice was clear, it had a warmth
Which one finds between friends
Yet, it had a certain ring of authority.

I had laid the groundwork for a debate
And I was prepared to follow the argument
Wherever it was taken.
It was a feeling of power; not arrogance,
But a feeling of knowing and of being willing to engage
In an examination of that knowledge.

TO THE COFFIN

I see you still,
Sitting and looking back at me,
Unblinking.
I believe you were
Not staring as much as trying
To take me into your awareness;
Trying to understand what had just happened
Between you, master, and myself.

We sat thus for several minutes
Until your head began to nod up and down very slowly
And your mouth – which until this time
Had not attracted my attention – began to smile;
A soft smile, which captured my eyes and
Caused my breath to quicken.
Oh, Abelard,
Did you notice these small things?

I knew in my heart
I had crossed a great divide –
A chasm which few had dared approach.

I waited for the riposte,
The thrust which would tell me
I had invaded or had drawn too close;
But, it never came.
Instead, your hand, palm upturned
Emerged from beneath your robe
Extended towards me.
I placed my own hand in yours
And so we sat, two immobile sensibilities;
The wind raging against the stone walls
Logs crackling and candles' light

Wavering across the walls.

HELOISE TO HERSELF

I could not bear the silence,
Could not bear that touch,
Prolonged past common courtesy,
Stretched in time beyond some unknown
Unnamed boundary which I had never known
And never broached.
I made to withdraw but found myself Held like
some hapless insect
By a cruel youth's pin or knife-point.

Our eyes were locked.

Mine closed,
Only when they dried and then
They were suddenly filled with hot, swelling tears,
Not tears of sorrow, nor pain;
Not those of laughter, nor joy;

But tears which come from the contemplation of perfection,
Tears I may say, of Grace.

Our studies proceeded.
As Autumn gave way to Winter
There were times of silent contemplation
But your incessant demand for understanding
All sides to an argument
Did, on more than one occasion,
Bring me to the point of frustration,
To the feelings of futility

Created by the attempt to make a point
Only to be invited
To consider slight amendments which,
 Once agreed to,
Became the Achilles,, heel of my argument.
Yet, I did not fall as vanquished.
Daily, my strength in rhetoric

16

And in the philosophy of ethics grew,
While my personal conflicts raged.

I yearned to know and to be known.
I knew no way to escape the role of student
Nor any way to quell an unfamiliar stirring.

TO THE COFFIN

How is an act to be judged?
A question put to me again and again.
How should we judge

The forger, the murderer, the adulterer?
Do the same standards apply to each?

And from whence do these standards arise?
Daily, nightly, we pursued these questions,
Dispensing with the standards set by the community
As being too ephemeral and subject to politics and geography.

More difficult to deal with
Were the standards set within Scripture.

Is an eye-for-an-eye truly a moral or ethical consideration?
I found myself doubting all that I had read,

All that had been taught me at the convent of Argenteuil
Where I had spent so many summers.

HELOISE TO HERSELF

I knew I was lost and at sea,
Longing for some rock on which to climb,
Some firm point from which to view the world.
Actually, some firm point
From which to view my own conduct
Which was becoming increasingly casual and familiar.

No longer did we play
The lord and supplicant.
More often, we sat together,
Our books spread before us,
Our shoulders touching.

I remember you would, tousle my hair
In a joking way
As though I were some furry pet
And would on rare occasion
Poke me gently in the ribs
Causing me to laugh and giggle like a small girl.
I knew and did not know,
Did not want to know,
The depths of passion
On which we sailed

And the storms which were yet to come.

TO THE COFFIN

The anchor which I sought
Came in the midst of a quarrel
In which you struck me on the cheek.
My small pain appeared nothing
Beside the anguish and mortification
Which showed on your face.

I nevertheless had some tears to wipe away,
Some caused by the sudden sharpness of the blow
Others caused by seeing you

In a new and frightening way.
You must have sensed this as well
For you hastened to hold my face in your hands
Assuring me you meant nothing by your action,
That it was only your frustration

And lack of skill as a tutor which prompted the act.

HELOISE TO HERSELF

Though I could not accept the act
I accepted the apology hastily given.
Uncertain of everything
That had gone before
I was strangely expectant
Of what was yet to come.

In his anger made physical
A new and strange intimacy
Had been created.

The energy released by that blow
Became a part of me.

TO THE COFFIN

"Was that", I remember asking, "an ethical thing to do?"
I went on, forgetting my shame, my anger and my pain.640
"My uncle gave you permission to strike me

As part of your teaching,
As part of my learning.

"What you did would, therefore, be acceptable to him.
He would judge it a correct and right thing to do.
Others might see your anger
As unfitting in someone of such stature;
And would find that you had erred; that you were not right
In behaving as you did.

For my part, I could not believe such force
Was needed to shape my mind

For I am not
And never was,
Rock upon which a sculptor hammers. "

And you, fully recovered
From the pain which you had caused us both
Nodded as I spoke, then offered me a new direction,
A new way of viewing and of assessing
The ethical nature of your act.

"I had no intention to hurt you", you said.
"In fact I had no conscious intention
To even strike out at you.
Lacking intention, there can be no right nor wrong."

HELOISE TO HERSELF

I sat fascinated.
Thru one deft stroke
The immorality surrounding your behaviour
Had been rectified.
The act was to be judged on the basis of intention,
Not on the basis of a standard set anywhere;
Not on whether it was ordained by Rome
Nor inscribed on Hebrew tablets.

Neither custom nor law entered into the equation.
Ethical considerations dissolved into the personal realm.
We should judge an act by knowing the actor's intention.
It was simple, profound and strangely liberating.

Suddenly the possibility of contact with you
For which I had been yearning became possible.
The morality of my fantasy had been resolved.
I had no need to judge its rightness nor wrongness
Based on anything or anyone else
Other than myself.

I felt a surge of power as I realized
That being selfish –
Not in the sense of taking from others for myself,
But in the sense of focusing on one's own needs and wants –
Could be truly freed from the dictates of the Church and,
If I may say so, from Heaven itself.

TO THE COFFIN

I leaned forward to you saying softly,
"If someone strikes you on the right cheek..." To which
you replied, "turn to him the other",
And you gathered me into your arms.

19

We held, kissed, and loved.
Where distance had been a part
Of our unspoken contract,
Intimacy now became our goal
And our very *raison d'être*.

How I long for that touch
That sense of being at one with you.
You well know, that
The ethics of intention Freed
me from guilt.
And at the same time,
Rendered me a prisoner of passion.

(HELOISE brandishes the manuscript above her head. Some pages fall but she takes no notice of them.)

And here we have an autobiography!
You describe
Those early days of our relationship

As a time in which our hands touched each other
More than they followed the words of our books;
And as a period in which

We explored the limits of sensuality
Far more than we examined
The prophets and sages of old.

All this in graphic detail
You shared with another,
And left the manuscript to history.

I professed my love to you Affirm
it still

Yet to see these words,
To see our lives,
Spelled out by the hand
Of some devout monk
Working in a scriptorium
Pains me beyond belief.
To receive this, a copy,
Not even in your hand

Opens the door to a dark part of my heart
I scarce know exists.
A part which solemn contemplation
Of Holy word represses;

A part which only in the solitude of the woods
Can be given voice.

HELOISE TO HERSELF

How is it that I should be discussed
My sounds of rapture described?
How is it that my touch, my kisses,
My body,
Should be laid bare in words?
To have these memories
Rekindled, not in remembrances
Nor verse directed to me
But in tales for public scrutiny.

TO THE COFFIN

Abelard, I moved from girl to woman,
From virgin to your courtesan
In a headlong rush within which

My only desire was to please you.
I did not feel debased by this,

Did not feel I was sacrificing in any way.
Far from it, for I saw in you
Passion of mind and body
And I became determined to support
All that which had already made you famous.

If you were here now in body
Would you have a reason
For stripping our lives so bare?

As we continued bringing passion and pleasure
To one another,
Do you remember how your focus was drawn away
From both your classes and your students?

It was said you repeated your lectures,
Gave half-answers
And that you were sharp
When you should have been generous.

You must know
Word of your behaviour went about the town
And shortly, our relationship was divined
By even the dullest of workmen
As being the cause
Of your decline.

HELOISE TO HERSELF

The one person who apparently did not hear
Or who heard but refused to believe these tales
Was my uncle Fulbert,

Choosing to maintain a belief
In my chastity
And to avoid the possibility
That sexuality was alive
Within his walls.
And so he continued to host his star boarder
And myself, his precocious niece.

TO THE COFFIN

I remember
Some evenings, by the fire
I took up my uncle's challenge

To match his wit and strategy
Across a weathered chess board.
And you, circling 'bout our table
Would with nods and winks
And gestures too small

For his unsuspecting eye Guide
me;
Deftly moving queen and pawn;
So in the end,
My uncle might claim victory
But by the slimmest margin,
Then slump exhausted,
Regarding me with disbelieving eyes.

HELOISE TO HERSELF

In this small deviance
We conspired;
Giving up the win
While losing nothing.

Like a meandering stream
Precise time is hard to capture in memory

But it was perhaps after two years, maybe less,
That my uncle walked unannounced
Into my chambers.

Before him was a nakedness and evidence
Which finally impressed upon him,

In a way that countless snickers and jibes had not,
That the poetry of love
Was alive, and was being lived.
It was a truth
He could not bear.
He staggered as someone run through with a blade,
Raged about the house,
Ran into the street, then returned
Throwing platters about the dining room,

And demanded you vacate our home immediately.
No words could defend our acts;
None were offered.
We scarce looked at each other.

TO THE COFFIN

Lodgings for you and Marcuse
Were soon obtained
And while the clergy and merchants,
Beggars and students,

Dustman and smithy looked on,
Books, parchments and instruments
Were solemnly carried along the street
Looking for all the world like a procession
Heralding an internment or execution.

As you left, that part of me Which
you had claimed,
Was torn from me
And I bled tears

As though my heart
Had been ripped from
Beneath my breast.

After that,
The crazed Fulbert
Calling me worse names
Than ever were visited
Upon the basest of sluts Seized
every opportunity
To publicly defame me;
And, when in his cups,

Debased me further
Through threats and blows.

You and I became fugitives
From the light;
We met in friends' homes
In vacant lodging rooms
And, may we both be forgiven,
Within the cloisters of the church
On Easter morn.

You can imagine how it pained me Beneath
my outward joy

To describe to you the facts
Which told me I was with child.

You responded with joyful words,
Clasped me to your chest

And fell upon your knees,
Tears coursing down your cheeks.

Strangely, you begged forgiveness,
But exclaimed our child would be
The fairest lady or
The most learned scholar;
The very embodiment
Of perfection.

HELOISE TO HERSELF

You acted quickly

To protect me and our child
From what would be

The certain madness of my uncle
On hearing of my condition.
Seizing a moment
When Fulbert was out of the house

You disguised me as a nun And
spirited me out of Paris Setting me
upon the road
To your sister-in-law"s in Brittany.

By horse and barge
I left Paris behind,
Wrapped in nun"s cloak
Which served to hide me
From the eyes of those
Who might recognize me.
But I was sick:

Sick with separation from my lover,
Sick with fear of what madness
My uncle might perpetrate,

Sick that the blessing of the child within
Should further disrupt our lives.
I know I should have been feeling blessed, Should have
been feeling my role as a woman Was being fulfilled;

Yet, that being which we had created And
which lived within me

Had become the cause of such intense loneliness I would
have welcomed eternal sleep.

TO THE COFFIN

I was shrouded in guilt and shame.
The very garment which shielded me
Was a symbol of vows taken,
Indeed, of a marriage to Christ.

Did you know I was struck with horror
That, to save myself and our child,
I believed I had committed a blasphemous act?

My intention could not be faulted –
To protect the miracle within me.
Therefore, I had not sinned.

Yet, a pall of guilt wrapped about me
As tightly as the night air.

You had taught me the principles of ethics
But they had not yet become new eyes
Through which to view my world

On that trip to safety

My love for you did not diminish
Yet somehow it changed.

I still felt passion, still feel it;
But I knew that your strength,
Your headlong rush to solutions
Would some day lead me

Or you, or both of us,
Into treacherous waters.
That knowledge hung above me

Like the sword of Damocles
Ready to sever something precious,
But I knew not what.
I stayed in Brittany
Growing large and despondent,
Generating new life
While grieving the loss
Of what had been so dear;
Bringing a son into the world
While desperately missing you, his father;
Feeling the swelling of my breasts
While the hole in my heart
Grew larger and deeper.

Then, in a final rush of fluids and blood,
In the scream of life
That ushered the newborn into our lives
I felt totally fulfilled
Yet utterly and absolutely alone.

HELOISE TO HERSELF

I was lost;
And in my mental and spiritual wandering
I called on God to help me to feel whole,
To do what was right in His eyes,
For this tiny part of us.
I had no rational sense,
No logical sequence of argument,
No dialectic
To guide me in what to do.

God did not answer;
And, in time, I found the face of God
Became yours
And I could only conjure conversation.

I slept little, nursed as best I could
And grew increasingly frightened
That the love
Which had brought us together
Would somehow suffer;
But if it did, I knew that it would not suffer
For anything of which I was conscious
Nor over which I had any control.

TO THE COFFIN

To your surprise,
I named the boy Astralabe,

Remembering that curiously complicated instrument
With which one sights the moon and stars
And tells location on Earth.

You had shown me such a mechanism
As we stood at the window
Looking up into the black void

In which the stars and constellations
Play out their eternal battles.
Your arms encircled me

As you adjusted the pieces of the device
And I fell back onto you.

I still feel your hands
Stroking my neck and
Running across my chest.
You carried me to lie
Upon the hearth, where we lay and loved.
So, in memory of that event
And with the image of our son

Being the centre of a universe all his own
I chose the name – Astralabe.

HELOISE TO HERSELF

After some months,
Marcuse brought me word
That I should return, alone.
Alone, leaving my babe to others?
I was torn as though placed upon the rack.
My mother's love bade me stay
To care for Astralabe;
My lover's needs and passion called me back.
It was a choice designed in Hell

One which squeezed my heart,
Parched my throat,

Left me numb and senseless, but obedient.
And in that obedience,
I totally surrendered my will.

TO THE COFFIN

I made my way back to Paris ,
Leaving our son in the care of his aunt and uncle.
Your manuscript tells
How you attempted to appease Fulbert,
Claiming you had only done
What any man in your position might do,
Given the charms with which you were surrounded.
You argued, like many another man,

That you had to some extent been seduced by me,
Much as the mighty Sampson had been.
I, not yet 20 years of age
Who knew nothing of men,
Had apparently become the author of this drama!

HELOISE TO HERSELF

The charge was not without some merit.
For the line between invitation and seduction

Is one which may easily be blurred.
When does a touch become a caress?
A hug, an embrace?

These are not philosophical questions
They are answered in living, not logic.

Having received word
That I was soon to arrive in Paris

You devised a scheme which you believed
Would secure you a pardon from Fulbert
And which would restore
The balance of right and wrong
Within the household.
Further, you write, you believed your scheme
Would set right any ethical questions
Which might have arisen
Concerning the behaviour
Of master toward student.

Your solution to these problems was three-fold.
First, you would abjectly apologize to Fulbert,

Something which the old man expected,
Second, you would provide a monetary gift
To atone in some tangible way for the damage done
To the old man's reputation -

That he had allowed his niece to be corrupted
Under his very roof -
And third, you would marry me,
Something far beyond anyone's expectation.

Hearing this,
My uncle graciously accepted the apology,
Eagerly received the handful of coin offered,
And, though astonished at the offer of marriage,
Agreed to it as well as to a caveat
Concerning the offer:
That it be kept secret.
In this way, you argued,
There would be no disgrace brought to his own name
For, while fornication by philosophers, teachers
And men of the cloth was acceptable
Marriage was quite another matter.

TO THE COFFIN

Married, you would be forbidden to teach.
Married, you might be excluded from high office
Within the university,
And further, you might not be eligible
For Papal appointment to the bishopry.

When at last I arrived at my uncle's home
You surprised me by being there.
You greeted me with open arms
Showered me with kisses;
Yet, when I rushed into your arms
And we embraced
I felt that while our kiss
Had the form of passion
It lacked a certain quality.

HELOISE TO HERSELF

That kiss was long and deep
And we both wept on seeing each other;
But my woman's heart told me
I was not being held by the same man
Who had fathered our child
Before a blazing fire
Which cast a heat
To match our own.

Without a trace of hesitation
You unveiled your plan to me.
 I demanded,
"Have I nothing to say in this?"

My uncle,
Fearing he might be seeing the end
Of that which would restore his dignity
In his own eyes,
Stepped forward to remind me
That marriage to such a renowned figure
Was far more than I might have expected;
That Abelard was showing me
A degree of respect
Seldom accorded to women and adulterers
Caught in similar circumstances.

I remember the issue of secrecy
Was casually mentioned.

And I recall hearing the blood roaring in my ears
And a deep blackness which closed in on my vision
As I looked at these two accomplices –
For so they seemed to me at that moment.

I saw before me
The ruin of a great man
Who would stoop to marriage
To disguise an inconvenient reality
That he had fathered a child -
By one of his students.

While he might still claim deference
As a logician without equal
He could not longer be esteemed
For having that rare quality of virginity
Nor could he claim to have shown
A modicum of propriety.

I saw the pettiness of my uncle
Who would allow his "precious princess,"
For that is what he called me
As he fondled me in my youth,
To be joined to a man merely to satisfy his own ego;
So that he could hold his head higher
When at Court or Church
Knowing a truth of which all others were ignorant.

All this flashed before me.
I threw myself against you,
Pounding on your chest,
Demanding you retract the offer.
An offer made not to me, I pointed out,
But to my uncle.
We parted soon after
And agreed to meet again the next day
To discuss the issue further.

TO THE COFFIN

That night
I read by candle light.
I read St. Paul and Seneca and Cicero.
I read and prayed and cried.
Not for myself but for you.
I could see at once that marriage,
In the eyes of many,
Including many in the Church
Would be the right thing to do.
Yet by Papal decree that year
Clergy were to renounce marriage
And those married
Should consider their union annulled.

In my eyes marriage would have been your ruin.
Oh, your intention was clear:
By pacifying Fulbert
It would make it possible for me
To remain to Paris,
To continue to enjoy
The benefits of my uncle's society
While at the same time,
Bestowing on me
What must have appeared to you
To be a reward or a goal
Sought by all young women.

I could not judge you nor your offer
As being anything but fair
From your perspective.
From my perspective
It was faulty, ill-considered and doomed.
While a marriage between us
Might be a successful one,
One which endured the normal strife
Of cohabitation,
It would destroy that which made you who you were.

HELOISE TO HERSELF

When one has monumental gifts
These are to be shared with all mankind,
Not with a single person
Such as a wife.
Being married,
Your movements would be constrained
And require you to be attentive to me
As a good husband should be.
I judged this would interfere
With your natural course
As teacher and scholar.

And, if it were discovered we were married
I should be condemned
By those who were deprived
Of your presence and intellectual leadership.

Being married,
And being a philosopher
Were basically incompatible I pointed out.
 "How", I asked, "could you devote
Your intellectual energies,
Your entire focus on a problem
Of deep complexity
When infants would be bawling
And children would be demanding
You play with them"?

I went further, protesting
That since philosophy
Is not an avocation
But a full time commitment,
I should suffer in my role as wife.
Without marrying me
We should have been free to come and go,
Or to sit quietly
Or to make boisterous love
Following the whims and needs
Of our spirits and bodies.
Marriage would place us
Within sight and reach of each other
Night and day;
And, while our passion was strong,
Continued contact might, in time,
Cool the fire which raged between us.
I was not willing to marry in order to lose
That which I had when we were merely fornicating.

TO THE COFFIN

Finally, you should well recall,
I pointed out that
Perhaps you felt
You were honoring me
By choosing to marry me
And call me "wife"!
In so doing,
You would have used the bonds
Of Church and state
To hold us together

Rather than the ties of the heart.
I said then, and repeat,
I should rather be known
As your whore than your wife;
For the one would be present in your bed
Through choice,
While the other would be there
Through custom, habit and obligation.

Through all of this,
To your credit,
You said little.

HELOISE TO HERSELF

When I was through
You sagged, and
For a moment
I believed I had won the day.
"Oh sweet", you said,

Gathering me up in your arms and
Lifting me off the floor,

"You have made such an eloquent case
Your wisdom in this matter is unassailable;
Yet, I so adore you, so treasure you,
I cannot bear the thought
You should someday tire of me,
Or, that when I have died - or sooner -
You should find another.
No, no, no. We shall wed."

TO THE COFFIN

"We shall wed", you said, or rather intoned.
Like a sentence from a judge;
And I, too tired to protest, acquiesced,
Dumbfounded that all my entreaties
Had done nothing more
Than unlock the beast of jealousy.
Allowing, once again,

Your will to prevail
While mine withdrew, exhausted.

HELOISE TO HERSELF

So, I became engaged.
Our marriage, hastily arranged,
Was attended by Fulbert,
Your man Marcuse,

Various close friends whom we had made in Paris
And a priest -- employed for the occasion by my uncle --
Whose face remained hidden within his cowl
Throughout the ceremony.
In the sight of God
He remained invisible to us;
Secrecy within a secret.
It was a paradox
Befitting the circumstance.
In the end, we were married and then,
To maintain the secrecy of the act,
Departed to our separate homes.

In the days,
More frequently in the nights
That followed,
We rekindled our ardor
And our love-making.
In the early mornings, when you left
You would steal away
Like some guilty school-boy or errant husband.

Fulbert,

Aware of the comings and goings
From my bed chamber,
Began to chafe at the knowledge
That the arrangement

To which he had agreed
Nevertheless deprived him
Of the public acknowledgment and approval
Which the marriage might bring
And the honor to him
Which would follow from this.

He had allowed his niece
To be seduced
Under his not-so-watchful eye
And this had happened within his house.

He began to see
That without making the marriage public
He would continue to live
Dishonored and mocked at every turn.

To right this matter
He began to intimate at first,
Then to announce publicly
That I had borne a child,
That Abelard and I had been married,
And that Abelard
Should now be considered
An honorable man.

In the town,
I was accosted regularly
By persons demanding to know
The truth of the story.
When I steadfastly denied it,
Not knowing my own uncle
Had been its author,
He demanded I acknowledge the truth
Of the union
And then he beat me.
Beat me about the hips and breast
So severely
I took to my bed
Sobbing until I thought
No more tears could come
And then, thinking about what had happened
In the name of love and marriage,
Began again to weep.

Fulbert, hearing me
And being unable to console me,
Suffered such guilt and remorse
He was unable to remain within his chambers
And left not only his home
But Paris altogether,
Telling his servants
He was going to the sea for his health.

Arriving the next night
And hearing of the abuse I had suffered
You used Fulbert,s absence as an opportunity
To spirit me away.
Again, dressed as a nun
To escape the notice of those who knew me,
I proceeded to the convent
At Argenteuil
Where the sisters welcomed me
And took me in
To comfort me as best they could.

TO THE COFFIN

The servants described how,
On my uncle's return
He discovered my absence
And that he heard from the housekeeper
That you had been instrumental
In my removal.

Screaming that placing me within the convent
Must have been your way to dispose of me
And that the whole marriage
Had been a sham,
Fulbert's temper once again erupted
And drove him near the point of madness.

In this state
He summoned both the faculty and the venom
To plan his next assault on you
And on our relationship.

HELOISE TO HERSELF

The shrouded priest,
No friend of the canon Fulbert
Yet willing to accept payment
To conduct the secret union
Came forth, unbidden,
To recount the sordid events
Revealed in Court,
Which to this day,
Fill me with terror, grief and sadness.

Within the very shadow of the church
A handful of coin,
Thrust into Marcuse's hand
As he left his Sunday worship,
Secured his treason.
While your landlord slept
That traitor unlocked his master's door
And bid three shadows enter.

Under Fulbert's direction
Two of his nephews,
Reeling from drink, fell upon my lord,
With a cord bound his privates tightly
In the same manner as sheep are rendered impotent
And with a single slash of the knife
Removed those organs
Which were the source
Of so much of our passion,
Our pleasure, and now our despair.

As they left your quarters
Your screams of anguish

Roused not only the household in which you lodged
But those in the entire court.
So many rushed into the street
And so impaired were the assailants
That they were quickly caught.
When word reached the mob
Of what had been done
The two of them were summarily blinded,
Cut as you had been,
And sent to stagger and bleed
Until they reached the canal
Into which both fell and sank.
Fulbert, recognized by some
As part of the assailants' kin,
Was chased
Until he took refuge in the chapel.

TO THE COFFIN

You recall how,
The next morning,
Such a crowd of students and town-folk
Gathered under your window
Expressing their outrage and sorrow
That the din caused as much pain
As the wound which you had suffered.
You called on Marcuse
To send them away
Or at least to quell their lamentations
But, when that wretch
Looked upon your bed,
Soaked as it was with blood,
He ran from the room
Joining Fulbert
In the sanctuary of the cathedral.

Their freedom was short-lived.
The bishops of the Church
And a cardinal
Visiting on Papal affairs
Convened a trial
And brought swift justice in God's name.
Fulbert's possessions
Were seized and given over to the Church
And like any common criminal
He was banished from Paris
And all its precincts.

To aid him
In finding his way about the countryside
He was given a lame ass
And a retinue
Consisting of a serving girl,
Who had not the gift of speech,
And the wicked Marcuse.

HELOISE TO HERSELF

In the convent,
At mass,
I was called out
To receive an urgent message
Which bore your seal.
I could not understand why
Marcuse had not delivered it
Nor why it should be sent
In such a secret manner.

In elaborate, flowing metaphor,
You described the felling of trees
The plucking of flowers by their stems,
The erosion of cliffs with time.
Finally, in plain and unadorned language
You described the events of that night
Asked I never think of you again
As being whole, or indeed
As being a man.

My shock overtook me;
Horror of the final image still envelops me.
My body shook
My mouth opened in silent scream
Unable to give voice
To rage, and pity, and the keening wail of grief.

There was more
Which I scarcely read
Through a screen of tears
Which refused to stop.

I was saddened to hear
How far from the position of canon
Fulbert had fallen
But could not grieve the loss of my uncle.
The single cut
Which he had caused you to be dealt
Had caused all my affection for him to be quashed.
All my girlhood memories
Of gifts, and play and pastries
Receded in mists most foul.

I arrived back in Paris
Within the week.
My head whirling.
Justice and fairness
Seemed to have been stood upon their heads.

TO THE COFFIN

Oh, Abelard, you lost,
Because of your marriage to me
That which other men lost through adultery.
I could not understand the rule of law,
Nor could I understand
The venomous way in which
God was treating one of his flock.

I could not leave you
Whom I continued to love so dearly,
Nor could I live with you,
For that would be tantamount to the marriage
Against which I had argued so strongly.
I was sick with doubt.
I knew only three things:
My love for you;
The physical pleasures which accompanied that love;
And the fact that such pleasures
Were undoubtedly denied us forever.

I was left with images and sensations
Of the past;
Desire in the present;
And uncertainty about the future.
I went to you expecting...I knew not what.

When we met,
You said nothing of your injury,
Though all the world spoke of it
In whispers behind your back.

You stood tall,
Overcoming whatever agony
This might have entailed
And held out your palms
That I might be received -
But not embraced.

I remember searching your face,
Looking for some sign
Of the warmth and closeness
Which had been there.
I saw only a smile
Such as that which graces the face of one's pastor
As he greets his congregation.
It is not a counterfeit smile;
Say that it exists independently
Of the person behind it.
In such manner you, my husband, received me.

You turned from me and,
As though we had had a long conversation,
Or perhaps even a debate,
Announced in a tone
Which you often used for a concluding argument,
"Therefore, you should return to the convent at Argenteuil
And take the veil.
They know you and you them.
You will be well received,
And you will find comfort
As a daughter of the Church and God."

You then again concluded aloud,
Although I had not been privy
To your inner debate or weighing of fact or fantasy,

"And I will become a monk,
Joining the brothers at St. Deny".

HELOISE TO HERSELF

I protested I had no vocation
For being a nun,
And could not see myself being a sister
Any more than I could see you being a brother.
"But" you said, "we shall both find comfort
Within the spiritual fold and shall be together in Christ".

I protested, amidst tears and sobs
We were already together,
Solemnly married
In the sight of God and man.

Nothing we did
Nor had done to
us,
Had dissolved this relationship.
I still loved you
And did not want to sacrifice our life together.

To every entreaty or plea,
To every rational view I put forward,
You stood fast;
Concluding our lives
As brother and sister
Were best lived out apart, serving God.
I should live a life of prayer and service;
You would continue your studies and work
In philosophy and religion
In the company of other scholars
Within the Church.

In the end, I agreed;
Not because I thought
There was any sanity to this direction
But through sheer exhaustion
And in obedience to your command.

I agreed to take the veil,
And that we should live apart,
Though I had not the slightest inclination to do so
Which might have stemmed
From religious contemplation
Or a desire to serve God.
It was your will I obeyed.

And so I went
To the convent at Argenteuil
And there began the process
Of destroying myself.
Whereas you
Had lost a vital part
Of your physical being
Before entering the Church,
I lost my soul
In the process of becoming a nun.

Perhaps it is extreme
Even untruthful
To say I lost my soul
But what should I call that process
By which belief in the supremacy of God
Is replaced by devotion and dedication
To man;
Not to mankind generally, but to *a* man,
A process in which the spiritual love of God
recedes And physical love ascends
To dominate one's thoughts and dreams.

Blasphemy?
The triumph of Lucifer?
Corruption?
What base name can be conjured up
That I have not already heard
From my own lips?
Yet, in my heart,
I never professed more
Than I have ever given.

TO THE COFFIN

You write to your unnamed friend
Of the solemnity
And majesty of the service
In which you consecrated your life to Christ.
You speak eloquently
About the sense of peace
Which descended over you
As you were accepted into the brother-hood.

For my part,
I recall only the burning tears
Which coursed down my cheeks
And the cold hard stone of the chapel floor
As I threw myself upon it
Before the altar
And allowed myself to succumb
To monastic rule.

Thus, I followed your command.
I change my robes and aligned myself
With God's daughters.
My body was directed
As surely as if you had trussed me up
And delivered me to the altar
Where my vows were taken.

While I profess to have an intellect,
A sensibility to nature,
And a command of languages
I was dumb in all of these
As I gave my body to the church.
But one thing could not be commanded;
Could not be controlled from without –
My passion and my love for you,

Whom I called my lover and my husband
And who in turn,
In letters exchanged between us
Addressed me as his sister.

That you referred to me
As your "Sister in Christ" pained me
Beyond measure.
Daily, nightly, I prayed
To religious icons of the Christ.
But, whereas my sisters believed
That through the Crucifix their prayers
Were lifted up to God,
My fervent hope was that my entreaties
Would be heard by you.

TO THE AUDIENCE

I had felt guilt when donning a nun's habit
To escape from harm.

And, even though the wearing of this garb
Has been legitimized through oath
I am daily immersed in guilt
For using prayer designed for God
To reach not Him but Abelard.

For several years I labored
In the service of my sisters
At Argenteuil.
Increasingly, these daughters of Christ,
Young and old, novice and abbess alike
Turned to me for guidance.
Where it was I who should have been asking for direction
I found myself implored to offer it.

When I might have been
In neighbouring villages
Collecting alms
For our humble existence,
I found myself
Negotiating with land-owners;
Pledging portions of crops;
Receiving Papal visitors;
And creating a most powerful corporation.
Without having training,
Much less inclination
I found myself elected
The abbess of our convent,
Advisor and leader in matters both spiritual and worldly.

I have proceeded in this manner,
Hearing now and then from travelers
Of your misfortunes.
In one church after another
You would find
The foulest of corruption and license;
Set about to remove this rot
Only to find yourself
The victim of plots to remove you,
Bodily at best,
Or to assassinate you
At worst.
Through chance or perhaps
Divine intervention stories abound of you
Surviving attempts at murder
When even the chalice was used
To carry poison to your lips.

Where some might use persuasion
Or resort to exhortation
To rid the clerical body
Of infection
I am sure you used scripture and logic,
The words of Aquinas
And, ultimately,
Visits to Rome
And ruthless Papal judgement.

So, you became hated,
Reviled, despised,
And where once students
Fought to sit with you,
You were now shunned by them,
Driven into the fields
And starved with your followers.

Other than these brief sad tales
I heard little about you for many years.
For so many, many years
I obeyed your command;
Did so in silence, without direction,
Did so because I had no choice
But to follow your dictates
Not because I was your wife
But because I could not refuse
Your will, your plan, your need,
That we should retreat from the world
By entering God's service.

HELOISE TO HERSELF

Was this also a path,
I wonder,
To retreat from one another?

Then, as God's will is done,
In the darkest hour
You became my rescuer.

I and my flock were quite suddenly
Turned out of the convent at Argenteuil.
An abbot who had acquired the property
Harbored great enmity for you
And, apparently, for those
With whom you had had an association
And exacted a cruel eviction.
For many months
We endured great hardship
Then suddenly you appeared

And offered us a new place of worship
One which you had built
Many years before
And named the Paraclette – the Comforter –
For you found refuge there while fleeing
From one of the groups of monks
Determined to put an end
To your attempts to rid the Church
Of vile corruption and blasphemy.

We gladly accepted the offer
And began our new life here.

While you gave the Paraclette to me
In perpetuity,
And had Papal approval and seal to do so
You remained our spiritual master,
One to whom we could turn
In matters affecting our prayer,
Our conduct of service,
And our personal lives.

TO THE COFFIN

So it was that you and I
Wrote many times to each other
On matters of interpreting the Benedictine Rule;
So that our assembly should know, for example,
How to correctly dress, since the Rule is silent on this
With respect to women.
I asked as well,
How we should treat male visitors to our abbey?
Should we dine and drink with them,
Risking the perils of wine and flattery,

Or should such guests be hosted separately?
And I urged you
To write prayers and Masses for us
As well as some song
So that we might benefit
From your insight and poetry.

In all these requests you obliged,
Even visiting us from time to time
To celebrate the Mass.

Yet, never did you so much
As pass a personal word,
Or word of recognition,
Of who we had been to one another.
Never did you allow me to speak openly
About my feelings
Never did you ask about our son, Astralabe.

Would you have been proud
As I was,
To know that our son
Wandering far off
In a canton of Switzerland
Joined a holy order;
Took the vows,
And now presides as abbot?
I yearn to see him

To hold him in a mother's warm embrace.
But, never did you ask,
And I,
unbidden,
Did not tell.

HELOISE TO HERSELF

In truth,
The human Abelard
Who held me close and who
Pledged himself to be with me

To infinity
Was no longer to be found.

The ecclesiastical, administrative Abelard
Who provided what we asked for
In all but personal respects
Was the only Abelard
With whom I talked.

TO THE COFFIN

Twelve years after
We took our vows
I wrote to you
Of my personal needs and desires.

I wrote of the hypocrisy I felt
At being spiritual mother to many
While feeling nothing for them
In comparison to the love
I continued to nurture for you.
I confessed that at Mass
When I should have been thinking
About our Lord and His sacrifice
My mind often drifted

To images and memories of our love making.
At night I found
That in my dreams
We often lay
together;
So close my body often responded
And I experienced again
The tremors and passion of our union.

I begged you to write to me
And tell me of your feelings;
To say whether you thought about us - ever.
I begged you to help me
Find a way to be truly honest
In my relationship to my vocation,
While at the same time,
Still joined to you in all ways
Save the facts that we did not live together
And never talked of our feelings.

Your reply came
As part of a letter of direction

Which answered many of my questions
Concerning the interpretation of the Rule.

The letter was addressed to "My sister in Christ,
From her brother in Christ"
And dealt with my plight

By commenting that
You thought I had the good sense
To solve the problem myself !

HELOISE TO HERSELF

This, from a man who stood
On the Olympian heights of my esteem;

From one who talked of the ethics of intention
And who made of me a woman,
Lavishing praise, wakening sensuality,
Even using force when needed
To satisfy his lust.

TO THE COFFIN

Oh yes, my love!
As Fulbert believed
It was fit and proper

That you beat me if I proved
An unwilling or tardy student.
So you too, through what logic
I cannot imagine
Turned to force

That you might gain entrance,
And so you did.

So blinded was I by my belief
In your ultimate love for me
I allowed it!
And through some aberration
Which I cannot fathom,
Forgot the event and later...
Desired you again.

(HELOISE tears some pages
from the manuscript, and
holding some in each fist
pounds on the coffin.)

And you write,
For all the world to know,
You were amazed at my uncle's simplicity;

And that, if he had entrusted a sheep
To a ravening wolf
It would not have surprised you more.
Was that the crux? The motivation?
That I should be ravished?
Was that your intention?
If so, then truly you did sin
And I am left defiled,
A consecrated sheep.

47

My love, like the passion of my body
Was not extinguished
By mere acts of climax.
My love grew and I nurtured it
With memory and hope.

How was I to use my good sense,
By which you meant
My thought and my logic
To undo this condition?
So great was my despair
That I could feel the emotional sea within me
Washing in waves that alternated
Between desire and anger,
Wanting to grab you
And to shake you
Until some of my passion
Should be thus infused into your body
And hopefully your heart.

But I could not maintain these dark feelings.
I fell back spent, defeated,
Still much in love
But in love with a ghost.
A ghost who still commanded me
But one which forever eluded me.

We gave ourselves
In what I believe was passion and love
Each to the other.
Yet, I may now ask whether
While I prized my lover
Was I but a prize for him?

In the end, *he* lost much as well:
Leadership within the community of scholars;
The adoration of students;
The affection of a son;
Being husband to myself, his wife.
Did he feel these?

TO THE COFFIN

Did you?
Did you feel,
Did you know?
In any way,
Other than to record the events?
Were there tears?
Longing? Anything?

When I heard
You had become gravely ill
Were, in fact, near death,
I wrote to the abbot at Chalon
Where you had last been given sanctuary.
I asked that the body of my master, my husband,
Be brought here, to the Paraclette,
To the last Comforter he would ever know.

I also asked
That a document of absolution be written
To be hung over your tomb,
And asked as well
If some position nearby
Could be found for Astralabe.

In the matter of a placement for Astralabe
Only a statement of good intention was received.
In the matter of an absolution
This was in good time delivered to me.
And in the matter of receiving your body
This too, has now come to pass.

But, I did not ask for *this*!

(HURLS the pages at the coffin)

Logic, the force
Which drove you to magnificent heights
Was untempered with consideration.
In the zeal to rid the Church
Of excess and corruption
Logic became the toxic element
Which left you hated by your brothers.

The passion for knowledge,
And purity within the Church,
Which had driven you,
Pulled you further and further
From the world of sensitivity.

When you lay dying
Not of the poisons served
By jealous and fearful monks;
As you lay in your last moments
Knowing it was but a short journey
To meet your Father, your Lord,
Were you still, in your own mind
The proud intellect,
Wrestling with the very fabric
Of our thought and souls?
Or, were you the humble eunuch,
Destroyed in body;
Your only family, a family of men;
Your lectures over;
Your letters to me rationed;
Your daily company a hymnal
And a crucifix?

In those last moments
Was greatness there,
Alive in the room,
Or was all that you had been
All that we had been,
A dimming memory?

(HELOISE falls to her knees as
Though in prayer – but with her
Eyes open.)

I am a Most Reverend Mother,
The daughter of Christ and the Abbess of the Paraclette.
I have succeeded in the Church
Yet I have failed God.

Indeed, I have sinned against You
Not because I did not do
What was asked of me
But because my intention
On arriving here
Was never
To serve a god,

But only to do the bidding
Of him, my partner,
Once united before You
In Holy matrimony.

(HELOISE rises, moves to the coffin
which she leans on with both
hands)

I see now -

That was no ordinary request
By a husband of his wife.

Perhaps that bidding
Which made me take the veil
Was born of fear, not love.

TO THE COFFIN

Fear that you
Should see me or hear of me
In the arms of another;
Fear that I should disappoint
And fail to honour our vows.

HELOISE TO HERSELF

And what of love?

What did I kindle in that frame
That could be so lightly shared
In public manuscript?

Reasons for marriage were given,
Foolishly accepted.
Yet not once did love become a part
Of his entreaties or design.

TO THE COFFIN

Your fears were groundless
But came from a place
Beneath your learning,
From a place
Of vulnerability.

I had no opportunity
To dress your wounds
Nor minister to *your* soul.
Instead, your command
Hurled me unwittingly and unprepared
Into the arms of Christ.

But, though the Church
May have embraced my body
My spirit has stood alone

Treasuring memories
Which I now see
Are no longer private.

You have shared yourself,
Shared me,
With the world.

You have used our lives
Our joys
And our pain
To comfort another.

So be it.

Yet - you have not lost me.

I remain yours;
Your wife, your friend, your lover,

Never your sister.

CURTAIN

BOXED IN

Notes

This is a fantasy piece I wrote on a very hot day, while nursing a glass of chilled Chardonnay. When I was much younger I used to enjoy all my drinks "on the rocks" but as my taste has matured I've realized that with the exception of some scotch, diluting drinks with "rocks" extends their life but detracts from their quality.

CHARACTERS

ERIC: 20-30 years old; somewhat "nerdy"; Should be wearing a white terry-cloth robe.

JOY: 20-30 years old; in a constant dream-like state; floats in and out of the present as she talks. Should also be wearing a white terry-cloth robe.

ERIC and JOY are each seated on the bottom of large boxes which have both the top and the front side (facing the audience) removed.

The boxes are side-by-side, centre stage. Optimally, these should be painted pure white, inside and out.

ERIC

Where did you come from?

JOY

Oh, a lot of places. For a while I think I was in the suburbs, then I got moved to the downtown area. I think I hung around there for maybe two or three days and then it was swoosh, right to here.

ERIC

Not me! For some reason I just got stalled at a bar right in the theatre district. I would have thought I'd go on like the rest but, just my good luck, I kept getting by-passed.

JOY

That must have hurt your feelings.

ERIC

Huh?

JOY

To be rejected. You know, like in an orphanage when they come to look at you but they pick the one who sleeps beside you.

ERIC

I guess. I never thought about it. I just settled down in between shake-ups and that's how I've been getting by.

JOY

I wish I had a place I could say I settled in. I've been on the run for what seems like years.

ERIC

Ever live in any swell places? You know, one of those tall condos or out on the lakeshore? Boy that would be something. Nothing but the finest around you and real appreciation for what you could add to the life there.

JOY

I was at a Bar Mitzvah once in a little Jewish mosque near the highway.

ERIC

It's a synagogue, not a mosque, sweetie. What did you do there? Just hang out.

JOY

No, silly. You have to work no matter where you are. I was part of the center-piece. A lot of people, especially the young guys, looked me over pretty well. One of them even touched me.

ERIC

Where?

JOY

In the rotunda, outside the dining room.

ERIC

No, I mean, if it isn't too personal, where did he touch you, your person?

JOY

On my bum, and one of my nips.

ERIC

And you could feel it? What did it feel like?

JOY

It was a nice warm feeling. Of course I didn't let him keep his finger there long.

ERIC

How did you stop him?

JOY

I fell over. Caused quite a commotion and the guy went back to his buddies and their drinks. I think it was on a dare that he poked me.

ERIC

That's almost being molested. So what were you, a little nymph, or a goddess or some character from the Old Testament?

JOY

I never did know who I was supposed to be but lots of us have been used that way. Rounded up and made to be part of someone else's celebration - without even knowing who we were or what we were.

ERIC

God, it's the ambiguity of our lives that really gets to me. Who am I? What am I here for? What will become of me?

JOY

You're sure a deep thinker. One thing's for certain. We don't ever disappear. Our form might change but what we're made of continues on - sometimes in different states but continues on, nevertheless.

ERIC

Let me ask you something. When you consider our current state, would you think that we've arrived?

JOY

Arrived?

ERIC

Yeah. Like is there anything higher? Like more evolved? Seems to me we're perfect in many ways.

JOY

I can't let myself go there. I don't know what perfect is. One thing I'm sure of is that as soon as I think I can settle down for a bit someone will jerk the rug out from under me and make me do things that I might never have done before; or send me places I really don't want to go.

ERIC

Yeah, I know what you mean. We might be eternal but we can sure be involved in some pretty shitty deals, if you know what I mean.

JOY

I do, and I don't think it's fair. Whole world depends on us and our kind and we get fought over but treated like dirt sometimes; other times left to sort of rot away. Disintegrate and evaporate into the air. Get carried across borders and dumped.

ERIC

Joy, have you noticed the temperature?

JOY

I didn't want to. Well, yes I have, but I didn't want to say anything about it.

ERIC

It's not too bad at first. You get used to it.

JOY

Does it take long?

ERIC

I never really timed it; but if no one comes for you I guess it's over with in about an hour, maybe a bit more.

JOY

I guess the light doesn't stay on, does it?

ERIC

No, soon as she closes the door it'll go off.

JOY

Maybe we'll be together for a while more.

ERIC

Yeah, like in the kids' lemonade...

JOY

...or the Dad's scotch...

ERIC

...or maybe...

JOY

...or maybe we can have a holiday for a while.

ERIC

Here in the freezer.

JOY

While we achieve perfection.

CURTAIN

KREON:
Based on Sophocles' "Antigone"

Notes:

There is a really excellent summary of the original Antigone (first performed in 441BC) on Wikipedia.[http://en.wikipedia.org/wiki/Antigone_(Sophocles)]. Since then, there have probably been hundreds, if not thousands, of different scripts and performances. This is "just" another one. Except, in the current version, Kreon – the king of Thebes – becomes the main protagonist and is shown to be absolutely rigid and to respect the rule of law far more than the dictates of his heart. In the end, he comes up short both as a father and as a ruler.

As in classical Greek drama, there is a Chorus represented here by however many actors/readers as the production budget will allow. Originally, there were 50 (masked) performers in the Chorus but this mob was reduced to 12 by the playwright Sophocles. It was the function of the Greek chorus to speak the unspeakable – the actors' inner thoughts, fears and motives and occasionally to challenge them. I have tried to maintain this function.

Readers may be shocked at the incest which is alluded to – but this is no more extreme than the recent behaviour of Woody Allen with respect to his step-daughter. Some of us have not moved very far from the thinking and behaviour of those in power 2400 years ago.

CHARACTERS (in order of appearance):

CHORUS: masked; almost always male.

KREON: King of Thebes.

EURYDICE: Queen of Thebes.

ANTIGONE: Kreon's oldest adopted niece, sister of Polyneices and Eteocles

HAEMON: Kreon's son, Antigone's fiancé.

POLYNEICES: The elder of Kreon's adopted twin sons – heir to the crown

ISMENE: Antigone's younger sister.

ETEOCLES: Polyneices' younger twin brother.

Sundry GUARDS and MESSENGERS

Scene I

(CHORUS , KREON and EURYDICE are walking in the palace courtyard)

CHORUS

    All the work not yet done.
    One's place in history undefined:
    Promises made to foreign shores, Treaties
    lying half undone. Wisdom, knowledge,
    and custom Balanced together
    To yield rationale, justification and argument.

    Judgment, impulse, intuition Learned skills
    or natural attributes?

KREON

    What does kingship demand?
    What does it need?
    Have I ruled wisely?
    In fact, I rule protected by the Guards
    The servants of the Senate.
    My enemies abound.

    Will they leave off and forgive me   Once
    the crown no longer rests Upon my
    sleepless head?

    Our nephews
    Shall be the death of me!
    Each demanding private consultations Night
    and day;
    Each peering into the Senate,
    Keeping notes

    Talking endlessly to tribunes, Guards,
    charioteers,
    Even to cooks and messengers.

    Their ceaseless inquiry about my days
    About the art of rule

    Has left me little time To do
    the tasks I must.

EURYDICE

    What two children could be more fortunate
    Than to have you as uncle?

    You have made them young men, these
    Sons of Oedipus and your sister Jocasta

KREON

    You might say as well
    Sons of their half-brother Oedipus
    And *his* mother Jocasta!

EURYDICE

    What moved the gods
    To have Oedipus slay his father,

    Marry his mother, and together with her
    Bring forth four children:
    Your twin nephews, and two nieces?

KREON

    Such confusion
    Is not for mortals to unravel.
    We gave them shelter,
    Taught them how to bear arms,
    Or to set a proper table;
    To ride or to sew;
    As befits their sex, and now
    The boys are grown to manhood –
    A state defined by the calendar
    And not by force of character.
    Now the fateful day arrives
    When one assumes the crown
    Removes from me the burden
    Of ruling Thebes

    As Oedipus their father did.
    Now the day is come when
    For one year, one will rule
    Until the other takes his place.

    Year-about the crown shall move
    A solemn celestial dance;

    Power and obligation,
    Rights and responsibilities,
    Treasury, army, navy
    All at one's bidding, all at one's door,

Demanding from the treasury.
I command, yet I am at their mercy
For if their loyalty be bought
Then corruption shall be the rule
And we shall be but pawns.

EURYDICE

And these two youth, schooled as they are,
Trained and groomed as soldiers, statesmen
Lawmakers and judges
Have they the wisdom to nurture Thebes
To lead the city and all its residents?

KREON

Though the calendar deems them men
They are in fact, but boys.

CHORUS

You were but sixteen when fate
Pronounced you fit to rule.

KREON

One will choose the kingship
Or the choice will be made by lot.

EURYDICE

Will the priests not intervene
And interpose divine will and wisdom?

KREON

The priests know only
The throwing of dice
And the reading of entrails.
They know nothing of statehood
Nor the measure of man which kingship needs.
But, I will flatter them, ask their advice,
Record it for posterity
And draft my own decrees.

CHORUS

    And will the archives show
    Which were words of state
    And which divine?

KREON

    In the end, the choice is between two equals
    Both untried, both without experience.
    Either of our own sons, Megareus and Haemon
    Would sit upon the throne
    With greater skill and grace.
    But, in truth, I have had to rein in both,
    Instructing them in the proper order of succession.

    They cannot understand, or will not accept,
    That my reign ends upon the morn.
    Neither will have claim but must
    Allow their cousins freedom
    To assume the burden as they will.
        (KREON and EURYDICE exit)

Scene 2

        (CHORUS to one side, ANTIGONE and HAEMON sitting close.)

CHORUS

    The fair Antigone
    Home now after being
    Her father's eyes.
    Guiding Oedipus for years
    About the fields and paths of Greece.
    Only a child
    But taking the lead;
    Caring, protecting, as best she could.
    Now returned to join her kin
    To fall in love with Kreon's son.
    A young woman now,
    With gifts of sight beyond the norm.

ANTIGONE

    Tomorrow, my brother
    Takes the crown.

HAEMON

    Tomorrow the crown Is given as it must be
    To one of the sons of Oedipus
    It has been thus decreed.

ANTIGONE

>Look how the moon.
>Hides behind the clouds;
>The crickets are still.
>In the distance Thor's lightning bolts
>Illuminate the hills and rumbling thunder
>Portends or trumpets tomorrow's birth

HAEMON

>Yes, birth of a new order.
>Yet, death of that which we know.
>Which of your brothers will take the crown
>And which by his silence
>Will wait the year,
>Withdrawing, watching, enduring?

ANTIGONE

>I have talked to each at length
>And then have pledged my silence.
>I say to you only my father's direction
>Will faithfully be followed,
>But both will take the crown.

HAEMON

>That cannot be!
>The directions are clear.
>One must ruler be
>While the other waits a year.

ANTIGONE

>Clarity of direction, dearest Haemon
>Is like a promissory note.
>While the intention is clear
>The execution may be faulty.
>>(ANTIGONE exits.)

>>(Next day, KREON enters.}

Scene 3

KREON

>So, the fated day is come
>A day foretold
>When a youth shall become a ruler
>And a ruler returned to common state.

HAEMON

    Father we stand here
    Grateful for your vision,
    All made stronger
    Through your guidance.

ANTIGONE

    We bless you, and call upon the gods
    To favour you
    With joy, long life and fond memories.

POLYNEICES

    Your leadership
    Shall be a model.

ISMENE

    Your strength
    Combined with certitude
    A goal to emulate.

POLYNEICES

    We, your loyal subjects
    Brought forth from
    Childhood games
    Salute your crown and soul.

EURYDICE

    Leave off such fawning,
    Lest the old man forget his duty,
    And his bond
    To that great king of whom you all share
    Heart and bone.
    The time has come
    To set the crown of Oedipus
    Upon his son.

KREON

    Enough, yes enough!
    Thebes shall rest in good hand
    If such sentiments be freely
    given
    To him who next will rule.
    A role freely chosen
    Supported by the gods,
    By the populace,
    By legend.
    Who first shall wear this crown,

Carry this sword,
Assume this heavy mantle?

POLYNEICES

As elder of the twins
The crown is mine
By right of birth.

ETEOCLES

And you shall have it
According to the law.

And once four seasons
Of the sun shall pass
In this same place
I shall assume your work
And continue to make safe
Our home and shores.

KREON

Well said.
But know that the crown is like surf's foam

Resting atop the surging sea
Which carves through rock
And carries history's ship and crew.

(KREON holds the crown forward to POLYNEICES who places his hands upon it
but does not actually take it)

CHORUS

History dictates
The present path
The future road
Is ours to
choose.

POLYNEICES

As king but newly crowned
I must give voice
To those dissenting views
That crowns are not
disposable
Neither are they so ephemeral
That like crops or fertile soil
They may be turned or tilled
According to the calendar.

CHORUS

    Oh Oedipus,
    So close, so close,
    To have your son upon the throne
    And through him rule
    As you once did.
    What is this impediment
    These rash dissentions made audible?
    Kreon hesitates, knowing well
    The temper of your son.

KREON

    If I understand ...
    You would flout the word of law?

POLYNEICES

    If the law be one which in its execution
    Should damage proper civic order
    Then, yes, good conscience would
    require
    I chose a path of common sense.

KREON

    You would reject that
    Which in your father's grief
    Was ordained
    Before he fled this throne
    Entrusting it to orderly succession?

POLYNEICES

    My murderous father
    Who plunged his wife's broach
    Into his own eyes when he learned of their
    Infamy went stumbling blindly
    Across the fields.
    He could not foresee nor know
    How weak his plan should be
    How weak...

      (KREON rips the crown from POLYNEICES's hand and places it on ETEOCLES's head.)

KREON

Now is our business concluded!
Long live our king, ETEOCLES.

(POLYNEICES draws his sword and waves it in the faces of all present.)

POLYNEICES

Look to your gates!
For I shall raise seven armies
Against you and on all sides
Will bring the force of justice
To right this wrong.
Neither rank nor blood
Nor past affection
Shall stay my sword.
The crown shall rest
Upon its proper place.
My head shall hold it high
And Thebes will honor it. (All
        but CHORUS exit.)

CHORUS

Two stones tossed upon a mirrored pond
Circles outward spreading
Each reflects a world unique
Until the ripples meet.
Then the rise and fall of each

Is multiplied until
Collision cancels out
The images
And leaves behind

The evidence of struggle.
The calm waters churn
And the reflected world is chaos.
        (CHORUS remains on stage, KREON is sitting, ISMENE wanders past.)

Scene 4

CHORUS

Eurydice bows before her king.
She grieves for the young children
Who played amidst her robes.

Polyneices and Eteocles are dead.
She will not lie with Kreon,
Will not make his rule seem right.
Will not spare forgiveness in the night.

KREON

Ismene, come, sit by me.
You move like gossamer,
Feet barely touching the cold stone floor.
Come, let me warm you.
And sitting by me give me some small comfort,
Some warmth of spirit.

ISMENE

Dear uncle, my liege,
I fear I may have wakened you.
Let me withdraw
And leave you undisturbed.

KREON

Oh, Ismene,
This night of all nights
Leave off with the "liege" and "lord"
Let me hold you to share your warmth.
I too, cannot sleep for I fear the dawn,

Fear your brothers' actions
Fear for your brothers' actions.

You are not a secret to me
I have fed you, dressed you,
Bathed you,
Given what I could.

Let me now for these few moments
Before the dawn
Hold you close

Ward off the spirits of the morning
Feel safe in loving arms.

CHORUS

Ismene, Ismene
Logic fights with heart.
Whatever risk there be,
Safety is a state of mind.

ISMENE

The whole world knows

I owe my life to you
What would you have me do?
To repay your generosity?

Your kindness?
Would you have me
Cross those lines of kinship
Which till now have made me safe?
The Gods know our stars
Are so crossed and double-crossed

That lineage becomes a circle
Beginning where it ends.

KREON

I meant only...

ISMENE

Uncle...Old man...Protector.
Reason bids me flee.
Pity, compassion, gratefulness

Root me to your side.
Come old man,
Let me give to you
And if, in the morning's glare
We see but folly
And momentary madness
In one another's eyes,
We shall at least remember
A moment's peace together;
And if we see a warmth
Beyond blood ties
We may smile and know

The legacy of Oedipus still lives
And we shall wait our time.

Scene 5

(The throne room in which guards are now stationed. KREON sits with his head
cradled in his hands as the GUARD speaks.)

GUARD

On all fronts my lord
Our brigades push back the enemy.
The din of battle shakes the earth
'Till the gods answer with rolling thunder
And the clash of steel on steel is counterpoint
To lightning flashing 'cross the Theban skies.
At our seven gates, our allies
Beat back those who attack

Ferret out those who infiltrate
And make our homes secure

KREON

This is good news.
I had feared more entries
In the roll of the dead;
More names of those who gave all,
Leaving all behind.
What of the traitor Polyneices

Who vowed to set the Theban crown
Upon his own seditious head?
And what of his brother Eteocles
Who took up spear and shield
Proclaiming an oath
That he should rid the land
Of those who would lead by treachery?

GUARD

Sir, as night fell
The field of battle grew still
Save for the cries of those

Whose bodies lay writhing
In mortal and final pain.
Only two men,
Some say grown large as giants,
Filled the landscape
Blotting out the setting sun.
Two men clashing,
Heaving one upon the other
Until their garments dripped
With sweat and pulsing crimson.
As darkness fell
So they two also fell. Each
had killed the ther,
Your nephews Polyneices and Eteocles.

CHORUS

Oh! Oh! Lamentation!
If both must die
Should the traitor die in combat
The patriot by his own hand?
Or should the patriot be killed
By the hand of his lethal brother?

KREON

No! They have *not* killed each other.

No! No! No!
Say that Eteocles has not perished
At the hand of Polynieces.
Say that the one, having killed the other,
Seeing what a monstrous deed
His strength had wrought,

Fell upon his own sword
Thus bleeding out
To become but a stain
Upon the field;

An image within our mind,
A memory.
Say that this is how it went!
Say that they have *not* killed each other.

In truth, it is fate which has killed them both
Through that weakness

Given them at birth by their father;
That lethal corruption of the spirit
Which turned son against father Now
turned brother against brother. Tell
me! I command you!

Who died first by the hand of his brother
And who next by his own hand?

GUARD

I cannot say, my master.
The truth is lost
Within the furor of battle
And the telling
From guard to guard.

KREON

You shall tell me!
You shall speak!
Shall fill my ears
With the truth

Of that which must prevail
To rescue me from torment.
By Zeus, you shall tell me!
Shall tell the world
Whether the traitor Polyneices
Fell first in battle or the patriot Eteocles.
The traitor should die before the patriot
Or justice is not served.

Each has sacrificed himself
The one to take by force

That which he coveted to hold alone,
The other to protect that which was his
By right of birth.
Now! Speak!

Or your throat opens one last time
Not to breathe again

But to let your foul
Spirit escape to Hades.

KREON

GUARD

My lord, how can I say

That of which I am ignorant?
Shall I create, on pain of death,
A fantasy?

A myth?
Praising one,

Condemning the other?
Had I been beside the pair

Heard the sword
Slice first the air
Then coverlet
Then skin and bone,
Then might I know
That which you demand.
How can I say in truth
The one slain
Had not offered himself
As a brave but foolish taunt
Hoping thereby to dupe
His brother into reckless attack?
When one is killed,
Standing so close that arms may encircle
One's executioner

Who shall say which is brave
And which the coward?
I dare not.
And if, for this uncertainty
I must die, I do so honorably.
I do not invite death but I shall not kneel
And wait for its arrival.

(Turns his back on KREON and exits)

KREON

You shall not face away!
Come back! I command you!
I, your king, demand your presence
That I may pass sentence.
Seize and detain him ...

He is gone?
Ah! Has bribery made him invisible
To the royal watchmen?

CHORUS
When power is thus defied
Royalty is most mystified.
A man who does not bow before his king
May be a fool
Or may, by standing tall
Reclaim a dignity
Lost within the servants' ranks.
(HAEMON enters.)

HAEMON
Father, let him be!
Give him pardon.
He is a simple guard, unschooled,
Speaking in the grip of terror.
Your might is not assailed.

Thebes remains at your feet.
Let him return to the ranks
Where he may spread his story -
Ending with your generosity

To hear him out
Then spare his life,

Though he had caused you
 Such misery and discontent.
Let him tell how
You accepted as truth
The unknown of the battlefield
Where slayer and slain

Know only blackness
And not the colour
Of their flags.

I shall alert the priests,
The augerers,
And the trumpeters.
Sadness requires propter ritual
To ease the heart
And send the fallen spirits
Heavenward.

KREON
No! You shall not!

HAEMON

     Father?

KREON

     You shall not ask
     Nor command on my behalf
     That preparations be made
     Nor prayers offered
     For those two
     Fallen as one.

     Let their bodies be separated, yes.
     The one, our beloved Eteocles,
     Shall be returned to us
     For all due state and temple rituals.
     The other, the traitorous
     Polyneices,
     Shall be left upon the field
     To rot, to provide flesh,
     Food for carrion beasts
     And the hawks of war.

CHORUS

     Hawks of war
     Screaming eagles
     Doves of peace
     All able to fly above mere mortals
     And see the trail gone by
     And a little, perhaps,
     Of the future paths
     Which men may take.
              (ANTIGONE enters and stands to one side, aghast.)

KREON

     Bring the patriot to us
     For royal burial.
     Leave the other
     For flies and maggots.
     On pain of death,

     That traitor shall not be moved,
     Nor be draped
     With royal cloth
     Nor anointed with wine
     Nor oil.

     And let the populace know
     That Kreon, their king
     Proclaims this; and add

That it is for the general good;
To establish order; to show the world that
Treason and treachery will not be tolerated
No matter the perpetrator or his station.

KREON

HAEMON

Father!
They are both kin!

KREON

And I am your king.
The traitor shall rot upon the plain.
Let his flesh fall
From his bones.

ANTIGONE

You speak as though
My brother
Was but a commoner
And not high-born as we.

Neither rank nor birth nor state
Reduces our obligation.

He is my brother – your nephew -
And your blood
Courses through his veins

As it does through mine
                    (KREON ignores her)

KREON

Bring the fallen general.
Accord him full honours.

We have lost one commander in battle
Another has but ...disappeared.

No records of his deeds Nor duties shall survive.
Bring the fallen general,
Thebes shall honor its son.
                    (GUARD enters shoving ANTIGONE before him.)

Scene 6

ANTIGONE

You need not wrench my arm! I
have not given cause
To treat me roughly, nor to injure me

The gods know punishment enough awaits me
Here in this capital seat of power.

KREON

    What is this unseemly action?
    Why do you hold her thus?
    Release her!
    Consider yourself a prisoner
    In her stead.

GUARD

    My lord,
    She was found upon the plain
    Amidst the carnage and the rubble
    Of recent battle.

KREON

    To wander 'midst the dead
    Or remnants of those who lived
    Is unseemly, but hardly warrants such apprehension.
    Has she stolen shields or plucked badges from the
    fallen?
    Have you?
    What is the meaning of this?
    Speak! I command you!

ANTIGONE

    Uncle, king,
    I was engaged in the ritual
    Which sisters must perform for brothers
    When death visits
    And leads them on their final voyage.

KREON

    You have tended to Polyneices?
    You have acted against my express prohibition?
    Have in some way treated his corpse
    With dignity, or in some way
    Marked his passing as one would
    A true soldier, or even a fallen peasant?

ANTIGONE

    I have provided what anyone deserves
    A cloth to shield his naked body from the sun
    A sprinkling of water for purification
    A covering of dust to mark the joining
    Of this world to that beyond.

KREON

So simple! A cloth, some drops of water,
A little dust.
You wretched slut!
You have defied the king
Broken his law
Treated the traitor as a human being.
If I had wanted that object to be honoured

To be accorded any vestige of respect I
should not have commanded
That he be left upon the field to rot.

That I have to some extent been successful
Is attested to by the complaints of citizens
Near and far
About the foulness in the air

And the screams of vultures which circle
Waiting until our guards depart
Before feasting on the spoils.

You miserable, conspiratorial wretch!
Did you not know of my decree?

It matters not - for ignorance of the law
Is no defense.

But, did you not know what penalty awaited
Those who might behave as you?

ANTIGONE

I knew full well that your decree,
Your law, your law of the state
Proscribed my actions and that
Severe penalties might ensue.
But the moral law which binds me

To my family, to my fallen brothers
Bade me go upon the field
And offer what I could to show
What reverence I could to Polyniece.

KREON

He has no name in this house
We will not hear it said aloud!

ANTIGONE

In my heart his name shall live forevermore.
Has yours closed a door
Upon that strapping youth with whom you jousted?
That small boy who rode with you across the plains?

KREON

Enough!

The penalty is death.
You acknowledged a death and now
You shall be married to it,
An eternal reward for a foolish act
Carried out in a momentary madness.
Take her away!
Tomorrow we shall take her to the hills
Where a cavern
Shall be her final bed chamber
Where she may welcome death, or not.
Whichever, it will come visiting
And gather her in its arms for violent union.

(GUARD leads ANTIGONE out without force and without resistance on her part. HAEMON enters from opposite wing.)

Scene 7

HAEMON

Was that not Antigone?

KREON

It was.

HAEMON

I should go after her
For we have much to talk about.
Our wedding plans go well
But need decisions
Which only she can make.

KREON

She has made enough decisions
For one day -
Or one life-time.

HAEMON

That is a strange comment, father.
Has she run afoul
Of some household rule?
Insulted, unwittingly I am sure,
Some dignitary or senator?

KREON

Insulted, yes; unwittingly, no.

HAEMON

     But I must know. Tell me the story.

KREON

     It is simple.
     Your Antigone has defied the law.
     Has defied me.
     Tomorrow she must pay the penalty.
     When treason erupts from within one's house
     There is no cure but to excise it
     As one does a boil or leech.

HAEMON

     Penalty? Excise it?
     Father, what are you saying?

KREON

     She has broken royal decree,
     That by which all Thebans
     High and low alike are bound.

HAEMON

     And of what is she charged?

KREON

     There is no charge, only fact.
     She has admitted to the shameful act.

HAEMON

     Enough of this guessing!
     What has she done
     That warrants such threat of violence?

KREON

     I expressly forbade
     Attention to the corpse of Polynieces.
     Said clearly before all
     And within her hearing
     As she has admitted,
     There shall be no recognition
     No ablution, no internment
     Of that enemy who once enjoyed our company.

HAEMON

But surely she is entitled...

KREON

...To that which is lawful
And to that only.

HAEMON

She follows the dictates of her heart
To do what is right.

KREON

It is my duty to establish
That which is right,
That which is for the benefit of all.

HAEMON

As king, you will not be moved.
As father,
Who blessed the choice
Of my bride-to-be,
Is there no compassion,
No heart, no compromise?

KREON

It pains me to take her from you
But you shall find other flowers to be plucked.
The needs of kin must be set aside
Or my rule shall suffer
And the rule of law shall vanish.

HAEMON

As I love you, so that passion
Can, within an eye-blink
Become white fury
And though this heart
Would have you hold me
So I would strike and strike again
To bend your will
To ask release of one who
Is no threat but whose actions
Came from love and deep respect.

KREON

You would "strike and strike again"?

You would set aside the *lack* of "deep respect"
Not for the dead,

But for me, the living?

Tomorrow at sunrise
Antigone will climb the hills
Behind this home and find
A new abode of rock and stone.

KREON

I am no traitor And
say, therefore,
"Long live the king!"

May your own life be blessed.
Yet, rulers have been known

To have their lusty lives
Cut short
By an archer's errant barb;

Or a stealthy blade Plunged
into a sleeping eye.

KREON

You threaten me?
        (HAEMON draws his sword but keeps it pointed to the floor.)

HAEMON

I must wait until the dawn
To see if my entreaties
Will reach your heart. (HAEMON exits)

KREON

This is my lot.
Commander, judge, and now, executioner.
Perhaps my son shall kill his father
As did Oedipus.

I must not fear that end
For living without law
Would kill our city state.
        (KREON Exits)

Scene 8

        (EURYDICE sits alone, sewing. ISMENE enters, racked with grief and stands
        with her one hand resting below her navel – as pregnant women sometimes
        do.)

ISMENE

Only we three?
Myself, your son Haemon
And the noble Kreon,

Are we the end of this proud family?
Your younger son Megareus
Close friend to Eteocles
Rushing joyously into battle,
Fiercely proud,
Wanting to right the wrong
Dealt our house by Polyneices;
But fell even while trumpets'
Battle knell announced
The opening charge.
My brothers, one lauded,
The other reviled,
Both also victims of the royal battle,
And my dear, sweet, Antigone
Dead within a rocky tomb.

EURYDICE

The gods have taken severe tributes from us,
Not given willingly
And grieved forever more.
You have lost your brothers and a sister.
From the same womb
There can be none closer.
From my womb
I gave forth two sons.
How much closer their bond,
Each to the other,
Than their ties to me?
Or, being their mother
Had I first place in their
Hearts?
It matters not.
We must collect ourselves,
Put on mourners' robes
Present strength to the city,
And save our grief for nightfall
Around our hearth.

CHORUS

And the public shall see
What strength you have

And will it wonder
Where your heart has hidden?
            (Enter KREON shoving a MESSENGER ahead of him.)

KREON
    Say it!
    Say it, that I should not!
    Say it!
    That the words be remembered
    As those from another
    And leave me clear of blame.
    But... no, do not say it
    As you would, reporting from the field.
    Say it that it may be heard,
    But... let the words fall...
    Gently.
MESSENGER

    My lord,
    There is no gentle voice
    That can soften the blow.
    Truth in any guise or voice
    May maim or pierce the heart
    As does the arrow or the lance.

EURYDICE
    My husband bade you speak
    Yet cautioned you
    To make soft the blow
    From that which would
    Harm our sensibilities.
    We, I, must know
    And you must be midwife
    To that news
    From which protection
    Must be sought.
MESSENGER

    My lady,
    Your husband lives
    Because your son Haemon
    Put down his sword
    When railing against
    The logic of the state,
    And the word of his king.
    So too, he found he could not

Bend his father's will,
And lost thereby his bride-to-be.
ISMENE

Did he not try to intercede
To stop the execution of the law,
To reason with the Court, his
father,
To save his love,
His future?

MESSENGER
My lady,
He arrived too late.
The guards posted 'round
Told how the king had helped to roll
The last great rock to seal the cave.
Your brother stood and offered prayers,
Tears welling up and flowing
Like an endless river.
Then, from within, from behind the rocks,
We heard faint prayers, crying and
lamentations.
Your sister's voice echoing within the cavern
Until sound, folding back on sound,
Created a whole CHORUS of pitiable sorrow.
Then, with one wrenching gasp
All became still.
Master Haemon toiled to roll back
That last obstacle to life
Which the king himself installed.
Too late.
All was still within.
The only sound heard then,
Some sheep along the hillsides
And the brushing grasses
To provided evidence of life.
And, seeing the fair Antigone swing slowly,
Hanged by her garments
Fashioned by her own hand
To make a rope,
Her life force
Squeezed to nought,
Haemon took again his sword
And plunged it
Through his heart.

(EURYDICE turns away and silently
exits.)

ISMENE

Haemon, dead?
Haemon, dead, too?
Oh, damn the blood
Which bathes this cursed house.
Damn that heroic weakness
Which takes one's own life
In the face of bitter loss.
I shall see to the queen
We are shortly to become
Nothing.
No one.
No royal house,
No legacy of once-famed greatness.
We are shortly to become
The stuff of tales
Impossible to believe;
Stories of the ravages of war.
Those left behind know nothing
Of the physical pain of battle
Yet suffer still, grow bitter,
And may revolt in the name of peace.
        (ISMENE exits. There is a SCREAM offstage)

KREON

I cannot look!
Such screams portend
The end of suffering
Yet, in that end
Is the beginning of another,
The suffering of guilt, of loss, of grief.
I dare not face
Whoever shall survive.
I have taken from each
All that they held dear.
                (To the MESSENGER)
Call in the priests.
                (MESSENGER exits.)
Call in the priests
That we may bury the last

88

Of my sister's issue.
Or, call in the priests
That we may bury the queen,
And, if that be so,
They may prepare the young Ismene
To rule as consort with me.

        (ISMENE enters, carrying a bloody knife.)

ISMENE

My lord,
She spoke only a few words
And those taut and strangled
As her breath ebbed,
Her dagger's handle
Pulsing and falling in piteous rhythm.
"Tell him", she said,
"The gods will have no room for him.
But Hades and the Furies
Shall rejoice in his coming.
And he shall not be alone,
For his beloved nephew POLYNEICES
Will, sword in hand, be waiting. "
With that, my lord,
She breathed no more.
And her eyes stared
Looking for the world that was,
Or the world that's yet to come.

KREON

Ismene...

ISMENE

My father and mother gave me life.
You rescued me when my mother,
Overwhelmed, ended hers;
And my father, wallowing in
Grief and shame
Could look no longer upon his home
And fled from sight.
Now, the wheel of Zeus
On which we mortals are formed
And later ground to dust
Has come 'round again.
If I am with child will you give it parentage?
Or will you now proclaim us,

Enemies of the State?
(ISMENE hands KREON the knife she has been carrying.)

KREON

ISMENE it is not you
Who is the enemy of State.
If you are with child
The gods will make him king
Or, she shall be the queen.
It is not you
Who is enemy of the state.
The crown I took from Oedipus
Conferred on me
The right to govern men.
To govern men by law
Or by the force of arms.
Or, to govern men
Through love and common cause.
The battlefield gives testimony
That men at arms
May fight for king
And in the end be victors;
But in his own house
That same king
Must bow.

CHORUS

On the field
When soldiers fall
So too, fall fathers, sons and brothers.
The vacancy around table
Is nothing when compared
To spaces left in lonely hearts:
The mother's anguish,
The father's sorrow.
No stately laws can intervene
To soothe or mend that loss.

KREON

I am not the enemy of the
State
Nor am I ally to my legacy.
I shall not be here to aid you
Nor play with the issue

Of our momentary passion.
Somewhere, in the fields of Greece
Your father still wanders blindly.
I will seek him,
And, finding him,

Will tell him stories of the greatness
Of his children -
All his children -
Who lived and died for principle
And though I think them mad
Zeus will recognize their hearts
And place them in the stars.

CHORUS

Eternal lights within the galaxies
Pinpoints of light to be wondered at
Sons, daughters, husbands, wives, gone.
Lives cut short;
Seldom with celebration
More often without deliberation
Save the principles or policies
Which drive our ruler's chariots.

At the blue clear water's edge
The Agean washes rocks and shells.

Children play, mothers watch,
And at night, look upon the stars
To see the future,
Or antiquity.

CURTAIN

ONCE UPON A TIME

The events in this play:

Never happened.....

......but, they could have.

*FATHER is reading a good-night story to his **very** precocious DAUGHTER, aged 5.*

FATHER
　　Once upon a time there were 3 bears.

DAUGHTER
　　Why 3? Why not 2 or 4 or 6-and-a-half?

FATHER
　　Couldn't be 6-and-a-half. You can't have half a bear.

DAUGHTER
　　So, what about 2 or 4?

FATHER
　　Well, you need 2 for the 2 parents in the story and then one more for the
　　Baby bear.

DAUGHTER
　　Could have 1 parent and 1 Baby bear, couldn't we?

FATHER
　　Sure, but the story is traditionally a Momma bear, a Poppa bear and a Baby
　　bear.

DAUGHTER
　　Oh!...Proceed!

FATHER
　　So, once upon a time...

DAUGHTER
　　...this is a fairy story, right?

FATHER
　　Yeah.

DAUGHTER
　　So let's have 3 and a half bears.

FATHER
　　How could you have a half-bear? You don't really mean like a Baby bear cut in
　　half do you?

DAUGHTER
　　No, silly Daddy! I mean the idea of a Baby bear - like the idea of a Momma bear
　　or the idea of a Poppa bear. So in my story we'll have 3 and a half ideas.

FATHER

I don't see anything wrong with that except I don't know what half an idea would be.

DAUGHTER

Sure you do, Daddy. It's like when you say to Mommy that she has half-baked ideas.

FATHER

Well, young lady, that's different. What I mean is that she has an idea but it isn't completely worked out. It's not fully formed.

DAUGHTER

Like it could be only half-formed?

FATHER

Half-formed. A half-formed idea?

DAUGHTER

So, let's begin again. OK?

FATHER

Once upon a time...

DAUGHTER

...there were 3 and half bears. (pause)

FATHER

'Night, my darling.

DAUGHTER

'Night, Daddy.

CURTAIN

THE MANN ACT

(A play with very long speeches which is perhaps best suited to a play-reading or
study group)

About the protagonist of this play, Jack Johnson

I believe one of the best sources of information about Johnson is Randy Roberts' biography, "Papa Jack: Jack Johnson and the Era of White Hopes" (1983). Not only was Johnson a real figure, he was bigger than life itself. Watch the 2004 PBS documentary "Unforgivable Blackness: The Rise and Fall of Jack Johnson". It's a documentary by filmmaker Ken Burns based on the nonfiction book of the same name by Geoffrey C. Ward.

Johnson has become a multi-media subject.

He was also the victim of incredible injustice perpetrated by the US Court system.

CHARACTERS

(in order of appearance)

JACK JOHNSON – Black, former heavyweight champion of the world

CAR SALESMAN – White, legitimate businessman selling costly autos

CONGRESSMAN – White, preferably from the Old South, drawl and all

JUDGE CARPENTER – White, Federal Court judge, very Conservative

CONGRESSMAN'S WIFE – White, lives in the shadow of her husband

REPORTER – White or Black, somewhat maniacal

YOUNG GIRL 1 – White, late teens or early 20s, immature

YOUNG GIRL 2 – see Girl 1

JACK LONDON – White, rugged newspaper man and outdoors type

YANK KENNY – Black boxer, alcoholic, far over the hill.

Many of the parts may be played by the same actors.

Center Stage, a lectern. Various bits of boxing paraphernalia could be hung or placed in the background: skipping rope, sparring gloves, running shoes. These should all be very old - turn of the 19th century.

JACK JOHNSON was a very tall black man with an incredible physique. He was a heavy-weight boxer, moved quickly on his feet and his hands were lightning fast. His speech carried overtones of the black South where he was born but it was surprisingly cultured, as were his tastes – poetry, philosophy, Mozart. He defied the early 1900's stereotypes of the black man.

The characters other than Johnson speak directly to the audience, never to him, and he does not acknowledge them or their comments.

JACK JOHNSON

I am Jack Johnson. More accurately, I am the spirit of Jack Johnson and I come here, inhabiting a body and given voice. It matters not whether the body is clothed in white or black or yellow skin; whether the body is that of a man or a woman, and it matters not what type of voice you hear.

What I will tell you is an open letter, and if I were being formal, I should address it to The President, The United States of America. I mean no disrespect by sharing the contents of this letter with you for my story is well known to those who follow the manly art of self defense; may even be known by sports historians and perhaps by the occasional scholar of law.

I will have a little to say about the law; about lawyers; and about judges. I will say some words about matters of morality, and of loyalty and of vice. But, mostly, I will talk about justice; and specifically, about injustice - about taking from a man what he must surely value most: his liberty. And in the taking of that precious commodity so may go his good name, if he has one; perhaps his possessions, if he has any, and his future.

I've been gone now for over 50 years - killed when I could not control my car and it left the road. But the events of which I will speak happened nearly a century ago – climaxing on June 4, 1913 - and I will dwell for some time on those events once I have painted the background.

CAR SALESMAN

Over the years I sold many cars to Papa Jack. One was silver plated and was recognized throughout many cities. Another was the finest Italian sports car which could be purchased. Mr. Johnson drove it often and he drove it very fast. Even in crowded cities he was apt to cut down the exhaust pipe so that he could be heard for blocks. Mr. Johnson had a passion for speed. When he was killed I had the feeling he left this earth exactly as he would have liked to – on the edge, top speed, defying the laws of gravity.

JACK JOHNSON

I should tell you, initially, that I have recounted everything you will hear to-day in my autobiography. I should also tell you that my life has been chronicled by others in books which deny certain events in my retelling of my own life. It has also been fictionalized in a stage play which in 1969 was good enough to win the Pulitzer Prize, the New York Drama Critics Circle prize and a Tony award, and in a movie based on the play. The play and movie carried the same title - "The Great White Hope" and it was a story not about a white man but about the *search* for a white man who could defeat me - the first black heavyweight champion of the world.

So, my spirit may have started out black, in a black man's body and it remains black to-day, but the spirit you see before you is a different kind of spirit, one which lives in all those who hunger for equality among their fellow men. To date I have not been successful in satisfying that spirit. Perhaps you will be moved to carry my case forward.

CONGRESSMAN

Over the decades unsuccessful attempts have been made to persuade the sitting President to grant Mr. Johnson a pardon. None of these has been successful. Most recently, it was argued that the first black president of the United States should pardon Mr. Johnson as an indication of how far we have come as a nation, and how far we still have to go. The matter is undecided.

JACK JOHNSON

You need to understand a point of law – actually a Federal act which came into force in the United States on July 1, 1910. That date is absolutely critical and you will hear it over and over in my recitation. The Act is referred to by three different names: the statute itself goes by the reference 18 USCS @ 2421; it is also known by the name of the name of its sponsor, congressman James Robert Mann – from which the Act gets its popular name, The Mann Act (that's m-a-n-n) , and finally we come to a name which says what it's all about, The White Slave Traffic Act.

The White Slave Traffic Act was a move on the part of the Federal government to regulate the sexual habits of the country. It stated that it was forbidden to transport women across state lines, and here I will quote from the act, "for the purpose of prostitution or debauchery, or for any other immoral purpose." Now, when I first heard of the Mann Act I thought it was a fine piece of irony that Congress should frame and

Act directed towards the practice of the oldest profession on earth – one which depends for its existence upon its popularity with men. I remember thinking, "this is an Act which will earn many lawyers their Sunday dinners, because I could not imagine how, in a Federal court, debauchery and immoral purposes were going to be defined clearly enough that the guilty could be separated from the unlucky.

JUDGE CARPENTER

The intent of the law is quite clear. Only those guilty of transgressing it will hide behind semantics or flexible wording.

JACK JOHNSON

I will digress here to say that some congressmen from across the Nation who usually travelled to Washington with their secretaries, must have thought carefully and then decided that taking their wives with them would be a prudent move – one which would remove temptation and also afford them satisfactions which if obtained in their previous manner might now be a Federal offense.

CONGRESSMAN'S WIFE

You know, I'm not sure I want to go on those trips with him. The capital can be so stuffy and I would have to leave our home and my children. Perhaps it's just as well to leave things as they are.

JACK JOHNSON

I was prosecuted and under the Mann Act. The trial at which this took place occurred in Chicago in 1913, as I have said. On the face of it one might conclude I had transported women across state lines for immoral or other illegal purposes. And here is the fine line: I did have sexual relations with women who travelled across state lines, sometimes with me and sometimes to meet me for that purpose. More of this later.

A few years before all this, in 1904, a Canadian heavyweight with the alias of Tommy Burns became the new champion of the world and I decided, after having many, many victories on the street and in the ring that I should challenge him. At that time, the profession of boxing had fallen out of favor with almost everyone except the sports writers and a few gaming people. That was probably a good thing because Burns was not as concerned about the colour line that separated blacks from whites – even in sports - than he was about how much money he would be guaranteed to fight for his title. He was not a very good boxer and having the world title on his head rather tarnished that prize.

For three years I chased Burns around the world, winning everywhere and building my reputation. I wanted to be sure he would get his wish – the promise of a really big payoff. All I had to do was get him to sign up for the fight. Well, Burns and I knocked out everyone who was any good in America and England and finally we both went to Australia. Finally, in 1908 he signed. I wanted things to be pleasant for Burns and I remember saying to a reporter, "How does he want it? Does he want it fast and willing? I'm his man in that case. Does he want it flat footed? Goodness, if he does, why I'm his man again. Anything to suit; but fast or slow, I'm going to win." The fact I knew he would lose his crown was my personal triumph even before we got into the ring.

CONGRESSMAN

In our investigations of the fight industry we were dismayed, as I am sure all fair-minded people will be, to discover in the majority of fights, in particular those related to a challenge for a weight division title, that the outcome was well known in advance. I am not saying that Messers Burns and Johnson were in collusion. I merely advance the proposition which will occur to many, that this is a possibility. Should the challenger win, the demand for a re-match would be extraordinary. Should the current champion prevail – and the odds apparently favour him - those involved in wagers on such events would want to give their clientele at least one more opportunity to recoup their losses.

JACK JOHNSON

The fight was held in Sydney on December 26 and after 14 rounds a subdued crowd of 20,000 patrons, mostly white, saw the end of their world. Me, a nigger from Galveston was the new champion. Now you have to know that the fight was stopped by police climbing into the ring to stop me from completely demolishing Mr. Burns. I could have ended it earlier but the cameras were rolling to record the event and there was no point making it a short film when a longer one would get more play at the box office. I punished that white man, I took my revenge for all the slurs and shady deals that had been made to get me to that ring and now I set forth to live the champion's life.

REPORTER

Burns allowed the colour line to dissolve for a payout of $30,000 and proceeded to lose the fight. Johnson won and pocketed only $5,000. But the new champ knew his fame was guaranteed to fill vaudeville houses everywhere.

JACK JOHNSON

As I look back I think I knew, somehow, that the very first thing I should do was to state my independence of colour. I could not, of course, change my own colour, but I took as a wife, Hattie McClay – a fine young white lady who looked every bit the queen in her furs and jewelry. Hattie had been in the shadows as we travelled from the States and I was determined that neither she nor I should shirk from the public view.

With my new title she filled the role of queen at my side and we set forth into our new world.

What was that world? It was a world of entertainment. I travelled as a vaudevillian putting on a show of boxing demonstrations, singing, dancing and playing my bass fiddle. Many were surprised to learn I was other than a boxer but for weeks audiences paid to sit and to applaud my skills. Being able to entertain both within and outside the ring was a huge benefit to me for there were times, later, when securing a fight proved difficult and there was always the need for cash.

I tell you this so that you will understand I was not intimidated by convention. I enjoyed female companionship and I found white women to be more to my taste than those of my own race. There are those who say I sought out white women as a deliberate affront to the white society which had harassed me all my boyhood and young adulthood. But, this is false. If I did affront, then it was without conscious intention to do so.

YOUNG GIRL 1
> You know what they say about black men.

YOUNG GIRL 2
> Is it true?

YOUNG GIRL 1
> That's what all my friends tell me.

JACK JOHNSON
> When we returned home to the U.S. I found a changed society. Everywhere, people streamed into boxing arenas or clubs. Everywhere,
> they were motivated to see the boxer whom they hoped would be the Great White Hope; the man who would take on the nigger Johnson and return the crown to its rightful place – atop a white man's head.

It is estimated that more than 300 young fighters from every walk of life, from every state, began what they hoped would be the path to a battle with me. Rail-splitters, woodsmen, shippers, gentlemen from clubs, all took turns beating each other, hoping to rise to the level of national prominence from which they could demand a match. Jim Jefferies, a former champion before Burns, was pressured to come out of retirement to massacre me.

REPORTER

Actually, in my eyes, Jefferies was still the real champion. He retired before Burns came on the scene and Burns never beat him in the ring. He never could have.

JACK JOHNSON

While waiting for Jefferies to decide whether he would oblige, I travelled about in one of my beautiful touring cars, or in railway state rooms, celebrating one victory after another. I had with me Etta, a white society lady who was now my new wife, and two ladies of easy virtue. These two white prostitutes, Belle and Hattie, stayed in a different hotel than Etta and I but were always available when I felt the need for their company.

Eventually, Jefferies made his decision and began the process of whittling almost 100 lbs off his frame. The match was billed as "the fight of the century" and was held in Reno 'though at first it was booked into San Francisco. However, California's governor made his views known in a letter to the attorney general in which he said, "The whole business is demoralizing to the youth of our state, corrupts public morals, is offensive to the senses of the great majority of our citizens, and should be abated as a public nuisance, and the offenders punished". Needless to say none of us wanted to be punished for doing something a large number of the public was willing to pay to see, so we moved our activities out of that state.

The fight ended in the 15th round. Someone from Jefferies' corner rushed into the ring and stopped it. I am told that just before this I had hit that white whale a series of 20 punches to his head and face but that he refused either to quit or to go down. I had my vengeance. I proved he wasn't the great white hope. The date was July 4, 1910.

My good friend, the novelist and sports writer Jack London, commented that I had given a new meaning to the name Boxing Day on December 26 when I destroyed Burns and that now I had used Independence Day to silence Jefferies and truly claim my place in boxing history.

JACK LONDON

Friend? Good friend? I don't recall ever having spoken to the man face-to-face. I saw him from ringside many times and I wrote pieces in which I commented favourably on his ability. But friend?

I learned much from Jack, including his advice on how to be truly original. He said boxers, like writers must put the stamp of "self" upon their work – a trade mark of far greater value than copyright. And so I have held to the view that my life, in and out of the ring, should honestly reflect that which I feel is true to my self. In love, in sex, in business and in the job of being myself who is black by birth but who refuses to think black or to behave white because history or custom expects or demands it.

I followed this match by going on a vaudeville tour. When in New York, Etta accompanied me and I was proud to introduce her as Mrs. Johnson. However, she refused to defer to me in a way I thought proper and I was forced to leave her behind from time to time. At my invitation, Belle joined me in Atlantic City and provided a much-needed refuge from the company of players and hangers-on. Curiously, Belle thought she could occupy the position of wife and became irrational when she discovered that there were many other women of her profession – and some who were without credentials – who spent time with me.

Of course, having had much time to herself while I was on the road, Etta managed to acquire a number of admirers and when I accused her of behaving no differently than I had, she spent an entire day sending telegrams to these friends of hers imploring them to write and tell me of her good character. The fact that it took an entire day to do so impressed me for the messages were all the same, only the many different addresses needed to be re-written. So great was the hatred of me by many whites that late in the year, in Pittsburgh, a Southerner came hunting for me and when he could not reach me, shot and killed a bystander who had protested the racial slurs being thrown in my direction.

The year ended with an unfortunate expression of my anger which sent Etta to hospital. While sympathizing with her and regretful of my lack of control, I took the opportunity to impress upon Belle the seriousness of my interests and tastes by taking her to the hospital to see Etta and to assess her injuries. Fortunately other friends interceded with Etta and no charges were laid against me for what, after all, was a domestic dispute.

Two years later I became a successful café owner – a grand salon which also provided rooms on the second floor for myself and others who might wish to relax. I employed a number of women at this time, some white and some black, who provided secretarial and other tasks necessary to the running of my establishment. In September, Etta, apparently suffering from a form of brain fever or low spirits took one of my guns and shot herself in the head. While it released her from her pain I myself was plunged into deep despair.

REPORTER

He might be able to whip anybody in the ring, but he isn't man enough to hold on to his woman.

CONGRESSMAN'S WIFE

His grief was overwhelming and his sobs told the story of a deep abiding love which was lost forever.

CONGRESSMAN

It is clear evidence that associations between the races cannot be carried to the extreme of intimacy.

JACK JOHNSON

Shortly before Etta's death, a Miss Lucille Cameron came to my attention and whereas Etta had been reserved and in some respects distant, Lucille was both warm and affectionate. Lucille was 18 when she arrived in Chicago from Minneapolis, and she had had experience with men of all stripes. I hired her as a business secretary and although she did not live with me her mother insisted she did and swore out warrants for my arrest on charges of abduction. I was arrested soon after and it is at this point that the government began its serious attack on my liberty. As I look back at it now that was the point in time when my government began its serious attack on the freedom of all who were coloured differently, or who believed or who spoke differently from the ruling majority. Now, recall that the Mann Act made it a Federal offence to transport women across state lines for immoral purposes. Lucille had indeed crossed a state line and we had become involved sexually. All that remained for the government to do was to prove I had transported her, or caused her to be transported, or induced her to travel for these carnal pursuits.

Once I began to understand the direction of the action against me I thought of Belle, Hattie, and innumerable others – many of whom I had taken, and many of whom had followed me across state lines throughout the country. Some of us had also journeyed to Toronto and to Montreal in pursuit of boxing matches and although the Mann Act was a US Federal act it was not a matter for extradition but it concerned me mightily.

In Chicago, my arrest led to scenes reminiscent of the South. Mobs milled about carrying placards that suggested I be hung. Newspaper men – mostly white but some black ones too – called for the severest of punishments for me. And in the offices of the District Attorney lists of my former associates were drawn up and no expense was spared in locating and interviewing persons who had worked for me or those I had slept with.

Lucille, of course, was a prime target but she would not bend to the demands and bullying of the agents sent to build a case against me. From her jail cell, she told them, "Yes, I crossed the state line to see Jack, but you have to do that because Chicago isn't in Minnesota and Minneapolis isn't in Illinois". And, she pointed out, she had used her own money to purchase her rail ticket to come and see me. The poor Federal agents saw what they thought was victory slip away behind the smile of that delightful child.

Some black folk thought I would be a symbol for them in their unending crusade for equality. "No, I told them," I am no symbol.. Further, "I am not a slave. I have a right to choose who my mate shall be without the dictation of any man. I have eyes and I have a heart, and when they fail to tell me who I shall have for mine I want to be put away in a lunatic asylum." And I meant it. I could assert my rights which I believed then, and still believe, to be universal. The city of Minneapolis, however, seeing that I had taken the notion of liberty further than they thought proper, banned the publication of my name in any public utterance and in Chicago, my nightclub was closed down. So, in the land of free speech I was unable to make my case in the press, unable to earn a living as an entrepreneur and unable to freely associate with a woman of my choice.

The FBI, working diligently to protect society and especially young white women launched a serious investigation into all my associations – romantic, commercial and otherwise – and before long focused on Belle. Word was about that I had, on several occasions, abused her both by word and hand. She appeared to be the acid test. I had travelled with her across state lines, I had relations with her, I was accused of beating her and of paying for her services. All these allegations and more became part of the indictment which was presented at trial. In Belle, the District Attorney and the FBI believed they had discovered the very woman which the Mann Act was designed to protect; and in me, they were certain they had unearthed the prime example of the type of man who exploits women for immoral purposes, frequently for financial gain.

And yet, there was a type of inconsistency in what the prosecution was aiming to prove and the laws under which it hoped to destroy me. Since the passage of the Mann Act the courts had determined that if a man – a sport, a business man, a politician – *regularly* travelled across state lines with a female companion with whom he had sex, then it could not be argued that he suddenly induced her to travel for the purposes of having sex. For these men, they simply continued to do what they had habitually done. Yet, here was I, behaving in exactly this same fashion but smeared and reviled.

The charge on which I was arrested and taken away in handcuffs, was that on August 10, 1910 I transported Belle from Pittsburgh to Chicago for the purposes of prostitution and debauchery, both of which were crimes against the peace and dignity of the United States. Of course, I also had the charge of abduction of Lucille hanging over me but in due time this was dropped and she was released from jail – the government having concluded that she was not a threat to national security and that the worst she might do was to find me and resume her wanton ways with me.

But here I was a magnet for racial hatred. It was hard to know whether I was more hated for having become a boxing champion and having done so by beating a white man – an act based in brutality, or for having married a white woman – an act based in tender emotions and caring.

I believe the answer was clearly revealed about this time and that it had nothing to do with the sport of boxing. In a speech to Congress I acquired new distinctions. It was said I was of villainous character and had atrocious qualities because I had married a white lady. The speaker was applauded loudly and was moved to continue his argument that there should be a constitutional amendment that would prevent white women from being corrupted by a strain of kinky-headed blood. The case against my marriage was so eloquent that I have committed it to memory,

"Intermarriage between whites and blacks is repulsive and averse to every sentiment of pure American spirit. It is abhorrent and repugnant to the very principles of a pure Saxon government. It is subversive to social peace. It is destructive of moral supremacy, and ultimately this slavery of white women to black beasts will bring this nation to a conflict as fatal and bloody as ever reddened the soil..."

Hearing this, I understood. The case against me was a case not limited by the provision of the Mann Act. I had ignited the fears of whites – not just the fear that their wives and daughters might be victim of some kinky-headed nigger, but that the whole social order was about to come undone and the country would descend into civil war. Whereas in the past it had been North versus South it was going to be white vs black this time and the forces of law and order were drawn up to protect the status quo. If justice had to be blinded – or at least made a little short-sighted then that was the price to be paid.

The indictment which took me to trial had 11 counts: aiding prostitution and debauchery, unlawful sexual intercourse and crimes against nature – mostly acts which were alleged to have occurred between Belle and me in late December, 1910. When confronted with this, I was overjoyed, for it seemed to me that on a technicality I should be at once freed and found innocent. The Mann Act came into force on July 1, 1910 but Belle and I had not travelled together, nor had she travelled to meet me at any time after July 1. In fact, we did not travel to see one another at any time during the whole of that year. Though I was a simple boxer, raised in poor circumstances and not formally educated in the law it seemed to me that acts which were committed prior to a law coming into force could not be illegal under that law. So, even if we had travelled in early 1910 we had committed nothing illegal. But here is where logic and the law, or at least logic and lawyers parted company.

For several months Belle was the government's prized witness and guest. While questioning her regularly they wined and dined her, kept her in hotels and tried to make sure she would be friendly to their case. For her part, Belle made the most of her situation, demanding special treatment and threatening to recant or to forget details of her encounters with me. One witness whom the government counted on to prove their charge of my crimes against nature was Yank Kenny. Yank was a huge human punching bag, nearly always drunk but sociable and he was one of my former sparring partners.

YANK KENNY

At one point at a training camp I used the room next to Jack and Belle. I heard Belle screaming that she would "do it" or "do anything" Jack asked of her if only he would stop beating her.

JACK JOHNSON

Without Yank's testimony, there was nothing and nobody to support the charges of crimes against nature. Unbelievably, and I believe to my good fortune, Yank wandered away from view just before the trial and the Feds were left with nothing and no one to support their case. All except Belle, of course, but the lawyers involved declined to ask her to describe her sexual behaviour with me and so we were spared that aspect of the trial.

JUDGE CARPENTER

I agree with counsel's decision to abandon that line of inquiry. Furthermore, all unsavoury details of the defendant's relations with women are ruled out of order.

JACK JOHNSON

Throughout the trial my lawyer repeatedly attempted to make the point that since the passage of the Mann Act I had not travelled with Belle, had not taken her across any state lines, had not been involved with her commercially ,had not broken any federal laws. And just as repeatedly, Judge Carpenter over-ruled the arguments and turned instead to the examination of my character and my behaviour. I was not pleased when my lawyer, believing he was helping me, pointed out that my profession put me into contact with all manner of shady and illicit men and women and the fact that I spent time with prostitutes was hardly surprising. They were attracted to me, he said, not only because of the strength of my personality and the fact I was a champion, but also by the considerable

sums of money which I earned and lavished on those about me. While this was true, I felt somewhat confused at being able to draw the line between the defense and the prosecution when it came to rescuing my image.

Hattie was brought before the jury and testified, as had another of her colleagues, Julia Allen, that I had wired Belle some money to travel from Pittsburgh to Chicago in late 1910. She also reported I had helped Belle to establish and furnish a location for her trade and that I had visited her there.

In my defense, I argued the money I had sent to Belle was in the nature of a gift to tide her over since she had lost her job. I stated I had given her money when she arrived in Chicago in order to help her with living expenses until she obtained a job as a stenographer, but I denied having asked her specifically to come to Chicago and had no knowledge that she practiced prostitution.

The evidence against me, my lawyer pointed out, was purely circumstantial. There was not one shred of proof that I had induced Belle to come to Chicago for the purposes of prostitution or that I had in any way profited from any arrangements she made with her clients. In short, I was neither an impresario nor a pimp.

By the end of the week the sorriest parade of witnesses had passed by: boxers, promoters, prostitutes, others down in their luck in one way or another. Judge Carpenter called them all "unfortunate people" and referred to Belle as an "abandoned woman", a "discarded mistress" and an "unfortunate creature".

JUDGE CARPENTER

The jury's should note that its task and the real issue at hand is to assess the defendant's intent. Did Mr. Johnson intend that Belle come to Chicago or that he should make money from her activities? The law does not apply solely to innocent girls. It is quite as much an offense against the Mann Act to transport a hardened, lost prostitute as it would be to transport a young girl, a virgin.

JACK JOHNSON

The jury went out and for several hours deliberated, trying to guess at what my motives, my intentions, might have been. They returned a verdict of guilty despite the fact that there was no physical evidence by which the charges could be proved. I was found guilty on the basis of what someone like me, with my history, must have been thinking and planning.

JUDGE CARPENTER

This defendant is one of the best know men of his race, and his example has been far-reaching. The court is bound to consider the position he occupies among his people. In view of these facts, this is a case that calls for more than a fine. The sentence is that the defendant be confined to the penitentiary for one year and one day and that he be fined $1000.

JACK JOHNSON

I have often reflected on that all-white jury and on the wisdom which they must have acquired while sitting at trial: to be able to discern a man's future intention based on his past behaviour. There were no issues of reasonable doubt; only the certitude that came with knowing that they reflected the will of the people.

If it is still the will of the people that I should be found guilty under an act which was not in force at the time of the alleged offence, then so be it. If logic and justice are to be served then another verdict should be considered.

CURTAIN

QUIT YOUR BEEFING!

The idea for this little play:

I had a cousin who worked downtown in Chicago. One evening, just leaving work, he saw a city bus slam on the brakes to avoid hitting something or someone and the rear doors came flying open. Along with the doors, a couple of people were thrown out of the bus to the pavement. One of them started to get up but was restrained by the other who said, "Don't be a jerk. Now we can sue the bastards".

This isn't about bus passengers. It's more about being faceless and being guided or manipulated by "the bastards".

As many adults as can fit on the stage would be an appropriate number for this play.

The lighting should be low and from the wings so that many people's faces are frequently obscured by shadow.

Slippers or soft socks are appropriate so that there is a minimum of sound from the stage other than the actors' voices. Throughout the play there is a very slow counterclockwise shuffle. From time to time one or more of the actors drifts off into the wing -stage right- so that near the end of the play only the five actors with speaking parts are left on the stage.

The location of the actors at the beginning of the play is pretty much random.

ACTOR 1

We've been waiting a long time, haven't we?

ACTOR 2

Speak for yourself!

ACTOR 1

I am.

ACTOR 2

So what do you mean "we"? "We've been waiting a long time".

ACTOR 3

Oh for God's sake. "We" can mean me, can't it?

ACTOR 2

Sure it can. I just don't want anyone taking it for granted that they can speak for me.

ACTOR 1

I want to start again. We seem to have gotten off to rocky start, haven't we?

ACTOR 2

There you go again! I wasn't off to a rocky start, that's why it's a bad thing to speak for others.

ACTOR 3

Let's not go through all of that again, OK?

ACTOR 4

Seems to me that as a peace-keeper you really didn't address the issue. It's a matter of people taking ownership of how they feel and what they experience and not laying it on others.

ACTOR 3

That's a load of malarkey.

ACTOR 4

What do you mean malarkey?

ACTOR 3

How could I be plainer? I mean crap! All that business about talking for one's self; taking ownership of one's feeling and experiences. That's a lot of crap. That's what I said.

ACTOR 1

Now we've been waiting even longer.

ACTOR 2

Now I can agree with you. First thing I heard when I got here was you saying we'd been waiting - well you know the rest.

ACTOR 4

If any of us disappeared would it make a difference to them? Do you think they would really care?

ACTOR 3

I'm not sure there really is a "they". All I know is that I was told to come here and wait until I was called upon to serve.

ACTOR 2

Serve what? Serve who?

ACTOR 3

I don't know. I figured I'd find out when my turn came.

ACTOR 1

And when would that be?

ACTOR 3

When my number came up, I guess.

ACTOR 5

You're all a bunch of idiots! Can't you see we've been duped. We've been told to come here to see how we would respond to the call. Would we come willingly or would we resist? It's all some kind of a research project.

ACTOR 1

You mean there really isn't any reason for us to stand around and wait?

ACTOR 5

I didn't say that. I think there's a deeper purpose here than meets the eye. We look like a pretty random bunch - like we represent the community as a whole. So I figure what we do will give them a pretty good idea of what they could expect if they really did have a situation. Would they get broad-scale support or would there be a lot of resistance?

ACTOR 2

What in hell are you talking about? What do you mean "situation"? What do you mean "broad-scale support"? What's this about "resistance"? You make it sound like someone is recruiting for a revolution. Is that what you're saying?

ACTOR 3

All I'm saying is that there are a whole lot of us here and no one seems to know any more than the other. Why would they want to bring us all together, anyways?

ACTOR 4

Where I come from no one just volunteers themselves to waste away waiting for something to happen. If you ask me this whole thing is a farce. I for one don't intend to put up with this much longer.

ACTOR 2

Me neither. I'm going to be out of here pretty damn soon if someone doesn't make some sense of this.

ACTOR 1

And what would make sense? To say that you were chosen because of some particular qualities you had? Or to say that you were here because of a random draw? Which would you prefer? Either way, you're here and there doesn't seem to be much you can do about it.

ACTOR 2

Maybe I can't, by myself; but if the lot of us put our minds to it and if our bodies followed our reason I'm sure we could, collectively, make a difference.

ACTOR 5

I'm telling you none of this is real. I mean none of this will make any difference in the grand scheme of things. To-morrow we'll all be back where we came from, none the worse for wear, and a little wiser having had this experience and having met one another.

ACTOR 2

Are you for real? The very air around us says that something is imminent; something that is really different from the usual run-of-the-mill daily events. Can't you see that?

ACTOR 3

Yeah, can't you?

ACTOR 4

We're not a focus group or a random sample for God's sake; and we have been chosen; of that I'm sure.

ACTOR 5

You'll see. To-morrow this will all be behind you and you'll think of to-day as just another milestone.

ACTOR 1

Milestones were used to mark off progress from one place to another. I know where I was but I don't know where I'm going and I sure don't like the way in which our numbers keep getting smaller.

ACTOR 2

Yeah. Where are the rest of the bunch who were here? Where did they go? And how come no one says anything when they leave? Actually they just look stunned. Kinda like there's no one home in behind their eye-balls, if you know what I mean.

ACTOR 3

You have a crude way of putting it but perhaps they've been spending more time looking around than we have - more time trying to understand what's up rather than all of this chattering we've been doing.

ACTOR 2

It's hard to resist the pull, you know. I'm sure you've felt it.

ACTOR 5

What pull are you talking about? There's no pull. I, for one, feel quite comfortable where we are. Whatever those others felt they needed to investigate is no concern of mine.

ACTOR 1

No, it's no concern of mine either, but I am interested in what's going on over there.

ACTOR 2

Seems to me you're splitting hairs, aren't you? I mean, what's the difference between something being of concern and being interested in it?

ACTOR 3 and ACTOR 4 slowly move away from the others and quietly make their way off stage right.

ACTOR 5

It's heavy you know, the air.

ACTOR 1

I've got to confess I feel pulled to follow the others. I can't say it's just a matter of curiosity; more like an instinctual thing; a kind of herd instinct, if you know what I mean.

ACTOR 1 drifts off towards stage right, motioning with head movements for ACTOR 2 to follow.

ACTOR 5 is left standing on stage, shuffling about, looking off into various directions and then settling down to face stage right.

ACTOR 5

I guess tomorrow may not be all I hoped for. I'm not really ready to go, even though the rest of them appear resigned to it. It's nice to know I wound up being among the finest - Grade A. I expect they use humane practices...and of course there are inspectors to be sure of that; but I have to repeat that I'm really not ready to go.

CURTAIN

THE PLEASURE OF PAIN

(A monologue/reading)

Caution to the reader

This monologue is profane. It contains scenes of sexuality and violence but it is not meant to be pornographic. I have tried to convey the story of a man whom I met many times. All of the events, except those surrounding the hanging are true. That is, they are accurate in terms of what he related to me.

I was encouraged to write this piece by a professor of the history of drama who felt that not enough was known about what some people – perhaps many – consider pleasurable in their intimate moments with one another.

Playwrights are encouraged to "write what they know". In this case I have written about a world of which I know nothing.

The **narrator** is a young man in his early 30s. He wears a plain t-shirt and denim jacket and jeans; no belt; no laces in his shoes.

He is working class without a lot of education but with a large working vocabulary. He speaks clearly and without any impediments and is fairly comfortable narrating this story to a reporter who remains unseen throughout the play. At times he shuffles about, twisting and turning as he recalls painful events in his story.

The **setting** is a very bleak prison cell – on death row. There is a plain table or bench with one or two weathered wooden chairs. If available, a steel toilet fastened to the wall should complete the "furnishings".

The **time of day** is immaterial and the choice of year is flexible. If the play is to be set in Canada, the date is 1962; if in the United States, then it is 1997 – the dates of the last executions by hanging in these two countries.

Scene 1

At rise the narrator is seated, leaning back and rocking slowly, with his feet up on the table.

So, you're the lucky stiff gets to do the authorized story of my life. I see by your letter that you really want to understand my side and to tell your readers about my feelings, about what really happened. Not that the story hasn't been told a dozen times but if you want to hear it from the horse's mouth well then I guess that's me.

Since the trial I've been reading a hell of a lot: why there's so much poverty in this country; why societies discriminate against minorities; that sort of thing.

Likely none of that is important from your point of view. Most important thing is that tomorrow they hang me.

I don't think anyone from town will be here; maybe another reporter, or that old geezer who was in court every day. Every day. Waited outside, rain or shine, winter and spring, just for a chance to sit and listen. He couldn't watch – blind as a bat; but he sat there, his head sort of forward and turned to the side – never moved the whole day. Just sat and listened.

So, tomorrow he'll get to listen to what happens. I guess about all he'll hear is the priest droning on in Latin, and maybe the warden will have something he has to say in the name of the court. Then, I guess there'll be some kind of bang when the trap opens and I go for my last trip. It'll be a short one and please God I won't know when it ends. Horrible thought, you know, that you'd be conscious at the end of the drop, with the rope tightening and ... Well, let's just hope all I hear is the beginning of a click as my neck gets rearranged.

Well, it's not what you'd call high entertainment but I understand a lot of townsfolk have been looking forward to tomorrow. Not to actually witnessing the end but to knowing that justice, or God's will or Nature has handed me what they think I deserve. Seems I stirred up a lot of anger and that a lot of people got pretty upset with me. In fact, seems as though people are far more upset about what happened before the actual event than they are about the end itself.

You know, this whole case is based on pleasure and how one goes about obtaining it. Of course, it's also about pain and how one goes about handling that, too. Now, I'm not one for lecturing or trying to change how people behave; or how they think or feel. I've never seen myself trying to lead a movement, or be a model or a leader. And I've never thought that what I did would in the least way, be of interest to anyone else. Up to a point, that is.

I knew that breaking into stores was wrong; that being drunk in a public place would, likely as not, to get me into trouble – or into jail for the night. I knew since I was a 'tad that you don't yell "Fire" in a crowded theatre, or foolish things like that. What I didn't know was that what I chose to do in private, with no one around, except those who wanted to be there, would cause such a ruckus. I guess I should have been smarter. I could understand if what I was doing was planning a bank robbery then the law might take a pretty dim view of that; and if I was writing obscene letters to the mayor then that might catch their attention. But, what I didn't figure on was that what I did to get pleasures for myself and my friends – without harming anyone else – would become something so many people were interested in.

Since you're interested in the story I'll tell it like it happened. Nothing fancy, just the way I remember it; the way it really was. The trouble is, anyone who could vouch for what I say isn't around. Mostly they died of old age – my parents, for example; or they've moved away, or they met with what the Court calls, "an untimely and tragic end". There's nothing I can say about the death of my kin except that I was sad for some of them, glad in the case of others. Moving away is something that people do all the time and I don't see how any of that is related to me, and the "untimely and tragic" part of the story is why I'm here so we'll get back to that, for sure.

I think I should clear up one thing. I don't regard myself as a pervert. Others do, so might you, and the lawyers and the newspapers made up their minds really early on that that's what I am – and probably always was. They went to great pains, interviewing, looking for old school chums, even digging into the school basement files. I was told they were looking for my early drawings, things that might have clues or evidence that I was bent even when I was a small fry. But, I don't see myself as bent, or perverted. I know I'm not a homo and no one ever accused me of that. Which, when you look at it is really funny since there were lots of afternoons down at the old mill, or evenings by the dock when two or three of us guys would kind of hang around and take turns holding onto each other or once in a while doing what we called "rub-a-dub-dub". When we got older we stopped doing this so much because we knew it was risky even though we also knew that every cop in town knew what we were doing and we also knew a lot of them had their own friends and did their own little dances.

So, technically, I did some homo things but frankly it scared me and I really didn't want to get beaten to a pulp by the local toughs if they thought I was queer in that way.

But that's ahead of myself. I need to start where I think it all started. I know you don't go around blaming your folks for your misfortunes – then again, they were the ones who were the responsible adults. You couldn't exactly ask a six-year old to pick out who he was going to be safe with and who would almost murder him, could you?

Point is, Mom and Dad did a lot of drinking when I was really young. Sometimes they would leave me with one of my sisters, but most often they'd have my aunt, Becky, come over and look after the bunch of us. Becky was my Mom's sister and she was gross. She was also mean. Mean as they come. Her idea of a fun time was to send us into closets or into the cellar and tell us to stay there until we absolutely had to come out to pee. First one out was the loser and whoever it was might get to the can before she caught up with him, might not. But whether you made it in time or not, she'd belt you for not being able to stay in the closet longer. I tell you she was nuts.

When I say "belt you" I mean just that. She had this wide belt with a big buckle and she'd snap it like a whip right across the backside – and not just once, either. Then, when she was done giving you her form of discipline and your backside was looking and feeling like a piece of hamburger she'd make you kiss her hand in appreciation for what she was doing to help you grow up properly. Marty, she was a cousin on my Dad's side who stayed with us, made the mistake of telling Mom and Dad what Becky was up to. They told her she shouldn't say bad things about people. Then they sent her over to Becky's to tell her what she had said to them and to beg forgiveness. Marty more or less stopped talking for that whole summer.

It's hard to think about Becky. What I really remember about her was how mixed up she made me feel. I'd be crying and hurting something awful and she'd be holding me, stroking my hair, hugging me, trying to calm me down and making me kiss her hands. And she'd stroke my face and brush my tears away, sometimes with her finger tips, sometimes with the tip of her nose, once even with her tongue. So I'd be hurting and she'd be making me feel better and I'd be putting my mouth in the palm of her hand or kissing her knuckles.

I don't know what she was up to but I know the feelings I get in my insides are all over the place when I think about those times. I guess it was a good thing that we didn't have to put up with her for too long. She got hit by a truck or something and we all went to her funeral. Marty and I sat together in the church and held hands and when most people 'round us started to cry we dug our nails into each other's palms until our own tears came. No one knew we were both happy as larks that Becky was on her way to somewhere. I don't think we understood exactly what being dead was all about but if Becky was in that coffin at the front of the church then we were pretty sure she wasn't coming back.

Marty and I got to spend a lot of time together and we got pretty close in a lot of ways. I didn't know whether she was cute or ugly, that didn't seem to matter although a lot of my friends said she was really smooth – whatever that meant. Thing was, Marty and I had a special connection that neither of us had with anyone else and I think that started right at the time of Becky's funeral. Next day, we talked about Becky and what she had been like and what she had done to us and I remember Marty saying that she was really glad there was no more Becky. Then she opened up her hand and showed me some marks in her palms which she said were from where I had dug my nails into her. I really didn't think I pressed that hard but I offered to let her dig into me in the same way. So she did and that did hurt a bit and when we saw what we had done to each other we laughed and kissed each other's palms and then we both began to cry. We held each other in a clumsy kind of way – the way little kids do when they're hugging - and after a while we started laughing and then crying again and then laughing some more.

So that's how Marty and I first really connected. Then her family moved away and I didn't see her again until a couple of years ago when she moved back and got a job at the plant. There were six or seven of us crowded into a booth at the steak house when she came in. 'Most everyone knew her and so we shifted about and she joined us for a couple of rounds. By closing, we'd all had several more rounds and it was clear that Marty could hold her own. We weren't high but we weren't exactly judge-sober when we left and I asked her whether she needed a ride home. She did and I was happy to oblige. One way or another, we wound up parked a couple of blocks from her place at the end of the street.

We actually sat for a long time, having some weed, not talking, just kind of being in one another's space. Then, almost at the same time, we said words to the effect that we had missed one another and, just in a teasing way she took my hand, pressed a nail into my palm and then kissed the spot. I couldn't resist doing the same to her and we had a good laugh. Then we sat for another minute or two before I reached over and just for fun, and not too hard, pinched her side.

I guess you could say that that was the beginning of a petting session; but it was a strange one. We really did explore one another's body – in a non-sexual way – by pinching, and stroking, even a little biting. And each time we found a place that was particularly tender or that seemed to produce a lot of feeling in the other person we'd press, or scrape or clench just long enough and hard enough that we could tell it caused a little pain and then we'd let up and more likely than not cover the area with our own mouth or lick it gently with our tongue.

You know, you're looking at me in the same way the cops did and the same way the judge and jury did. Just remember, everything I've told you is about legal things being done by consenting adults.

Anyways, I don't know how long we kept this up but at some point I realized I was really getting turned on, and I think Marty was too, and we just stopped and looked at each other. Not just a quick look, but I mean really deeply into each other. I knew we could have sex then and there or go back to her place or mine but that didn't seem to be what either of us was going for at that moment. I think we recognized that there was something else going on but we couldn't say what and we really didn't try to talk, except for saying good-night and see-you.

Well, we did see each other again; lots of times. Mostly we'd spend the evening or maybe even a full day on the week-end going to the show or sitting around having a beer, or sometimes we'd go for long walks and then wind up at her apartment. And then we'd make love with no sex. We'd stroke and massage each other. There was no part of the body that was off limits. Sometimes we'd light candles, sometimes we'd be in total darkness and sometimes we'd use fancy oils or powder on each other. When I say there was no sex I mean there was no penetration of either of us but that doesn't mean that we weren't aroused or that we didn't have climaxes. It's just that we could experience incredible tensions and releases through our touch and sight and smells and even the sounds we made as we pleasured one another. And I don't mean to suggest by using the word pleasure that it was all gentle. At times we were rough and we knew we were causing pain but we each accepted this – in fact the pain became an important part of what we did with each other and we invited it. It became part of the pleasure we were experiencing with each other.

Once in a while we'd talk about how being with one another was so different than being with others. That was really hard. Thinking about her with other guys and then imagining what it was like for her, what they'd done together. But she kept telling me what we were doing was new for her and she wanted it to be just between the two of us.

When I wasn't with her, my mind always wandered back to her and to our time together. When I wasn't in contact with her, physically next to her, it felt as though my skin was going to explode. I don't know if it was a burning feeling or an incredible itch but it got so I needed her and couldn't wait until we could be together again.

From time to time Marty wouldn't be able to keep a date with me or she wouldn't make a date with me for a specific time. The first time this happened I felt panic. My mind raced and I could actually hear the blood pumping in my ears. I had images of her with someone else. I felt as though I was going crazy. Then, the next time we were together, she would explain the who and the what of it and I felt better. But the next time it was the same; being without her - or even thinking I would be without her - caused panic and I wanted her even more desperately.

The worst part of what was happening to us was that we each knew we were reaching some kind of limit. We found ourselves wanting more and more and our loving – our form of love-making – drew us into a powerful bond. I got to believe I couldn't live without her; she found that even when she tried to be with others, her mind and her fantasies were about me. When we were together we breathed as one, we took satisfaction in the same things and fantasies. At times we each found that we experienced a kind of blending with the other. I was her; she was me. We were one for a while, then struggled to become two separate persons, only to plunge back across our boundaries into the other. It was obvious that we couldn't know exactly what the other felt but we knew that below our differences we were the same in our love of pain.

I asked her once if she would still want to be with me if I didn't cause her any pain. She said she didn't think so because when she was in pain she knew she was alive. When she was with others – or with me– and there wasn't any pain, she knew she was living but she couldn't wait until she could have a truly intense feeling in her body. I told her I felt the same way and that sometimes when I was feeling really alone or low I'd give myself a burn with my cigarette. That seemed to snap me into feeling better.

This business of not being able to be without Marty, led me to wanting a guarantee from her that we would always be together. The first time I asked her for this she went deathly quiet for a long time and then she wanted to know if that was my way of asking her to marry me. I'd never thought about it in those terms but without reflecting on it I said yes, that's what I wanted, a lifetime together with her. I said I'd look after her, give her what she needed and would be faithful to her in every way.

Looking back at that discussion I think the next minute or two felt like hours to me. I wasn't ready when Marty finally said that she might want to marry me but she couldn't promise to be faithful. In her view having other guys in her life was a natural way to be and on top of that she felt that when she spent time with others it kept my own interest up and made sure I continued to want her.

If she'd wanted to drive me crazy she couldn't have found a better way. I was hurt, crushed, angry to the point I wanted to really savage her and when I realized how much she had come to mean to me I felt utterly powerless. I blurted out that if only she would not leave me I would do anything for her. I'm not sure where the idea came from but I offered – if she would have me – to be her slave. And that's how we came to a new sort of relationship.

A little while later we moved in together and when we were out in public I did everything for her without going overboard and being too obvious. When we were home I acted the slave role: fetching things, cleaning, even helping her to dress when she wanted me to do that. And in a true Master-Slave way she dominated me and I accepted whatever she asked or gave. There were beatings, mostly by her of me although at times she would command I hit her as well. There were scenes in which I was humiliated and scenes in which I was asked to be loving and kind and gentle. I did all that was asked of me. I could do nothing else. I belonged to Marty, it was that simple.

Don't look so shocked; or is that outrage? What's the matter with being owned? Does it make you less of a person? Less of a man? What's wrong with owning someone? Does it make you less of a person? Less of a woman? If you freely chose to be the property of another person is that a sin or a crime? Marty and I never talked about this together but somehow we knew that the scenes we were playing belonged in a much larger play and that what we were doing was something much bigger than the "love, honour and obey" script. We were exploring what it meant to be truly loyal to another person. We didn't feel we had lost anything that made us persons. In fact, it was the opposite. We had found a way in which Marty could feel powerful and cared for and I could feel safe, knowing I was doing what she wanted.

The prison psychiatrist wanted to know if I felt I had freely chosen my role or was I forced into it because of the fear I'd lose Marty. In other words, did she blackmail me? Absolutely, I told him. Every day I paid a ransom of duty to her and every day she gave me what I wanted: the chance to be together with her. And it went on that way for nearly eight or nine months until Marty announced she was getting bored with me and that I had become just so much fly shit on the wall. I protested and offered to re-double my efforts, asked her to point out how I could serve her better, pleaded with her to beat me if I failed to please her or beat me if she would get pleasure from doing that for no good reason.

I guess she saw how much her comments had upset me and for a while she dropped her Master position, put aside the small whip that she had started to flick at me and took me back into her bed. And for a while we were close again. It was as though the Master-Slave relationship had become a true bond that we both recognized. Then, disaster – that's the only word I have for it.

Marty announced she was tiring of us the way we were. There was no excitement in what we were doing together, no energy in our lives and that we had become what she had always dreaded – a couple. Worse than that – a couple that looked married. And she had a solution to this. She wouldn't leave me and she wouldn't ask me to leave. Instead, she wanted to change the terms of our relationship so that each of us was free to see other people – provided we did so with the other present. She wasn't interested in kinky, three-way sex or anything like that. What she wanted was for us to be able to have three-person dates. Sometimes she would have the date and I would be there in the background, other times it would be my date and she would play tag-along. I thought the idea was crazy and told her so but she insisted and so I decided to go along with it.

Mary's first date with me tagging along as her good friend – everyone knew we'd been living together for nearly a year by now – turned into something I could never have imagined. We went out for dinner, shot some pool and then came back to the apartment for drinks. It was pretty clear that her date had more than drinks in mind and he kept suggesting I get lost. Marty played him along like a professional angler; reeling him in, letting him run, finally pulling him real close. I couldn't take it any longer and left. Every nerve in my body hurt. My heart hurt and I was shaking. I couldn't remember being in so much pain and I remember seeing Marty look at me with a wicked smile as I lurched out the door.

The next morning when I came back Marty was sitting at the table with her face and hands all banged up. She looked awful but at the same time she looked really pleased. It took a while for me to get it out of her but she finally admitted that she had set me up so that I would feel the pain of separation but that it would be me who would choose to separate. She made the point that I could have chosen to stay but that instead I left. For her, the rest of the evening was a nightmare and she fought off being raped and now had no feelings about her ordeal. Actually, aside from the little pleasure she got from manipulating me, the whole evening had been a bore for her and she didn't want to repeat it.

So, there we were. Marty was still bored, I was still willing to do anything to please her and to keep her with me and the word was out that we were a sick couple and that Marty was a royal tease. We became hermits and except for going to work we kept pretty much to ourselves. That was easy for me – I did graphic design - and Marty was still at the plant working the early shift so she hardly saw anyone on the way there and only a few people coming home.

You might think that after our dating episode we'd be happy with one another but the fact is we weren't. Marty kept looking at me as though I was supposed to make something happen – anything to get some juice going. I kept looking at Marty waiting for her to say she'd had enough of being alone with me. But one of the things that was going on was that in our boredom we began experimenting with the whole pleasure-pain business.

It didn't take long to discover that a very small switch, applied many times to the same area, could create incredibly intense feelings. They're so intense that you don't know whether to laugh or cry with each hit. And, when you've had enough, and you want desperately to stop it's almost impossible. You'd think that would be true if you were on the receiving end but we found that if you were the one doing the hitting it could also be true. It became almost impossible to stop – you knew you were hurting the other but you also knew you were giving pleasure when each stoke that caused pain also caused the opposite. It was also crazy that when you were being hit you wanted, actually you needed, to thank the person doing the hitting.

And that's the way it was. We became tied into one another in a completely crazy game in which we were each more important to the other than anyone else had ever been in our lives. We couldn't wait to see each other, to say how much we wanted each other, to be the centre of one another's consciousness. I think we went mad several times and we hid our small, bruised, raw areas as private badges that showed how much we were devoted to each other.

It's not possible, I hear you saying, that anything like whipping each other could be the thing that kept the two of you together, and you'd be right. The thing that really kept us together turned out to be a really old fashioned thing called love. I didn't have a clue as to what my real feelings were for Marty until I went a little overboard with the flogging one night and didn't hear her safe word. I kept it up even though she was telling me over and over that we'd hit her limit – and then some. It was a simple expression, "End It !" but I didn't hear her and she got hurt. Not the hurt she wanted and enjoyed, I mean really way beyond that.

When I realized what I'd done I thought I would literally die and for the first time the connection between us completely unraveled. She couldn't believe I had behaved so cruelly, and thought I meant to hurt her; saw me as being a sadist – not a partner. I saw her as a terribly wounded little bird who had lost all trust in me. I wanted to pick her up and heal her, make everything OK, make her see that we'd had an accident but that everything was still good between us.

When there was nothing coming from her to me everything I was went out from me to her. For the first time I wanted nothing from her; didn't want to hear her say she'd be with me forever; or that she'd marry me, or that she couldn't live without me. All I wanted was to hold her and help her feel safe. I wanted everything for her and would have given everything I had to make her feel whole and well.

She must have known something in me changed because after she healed – maybe three or four weeks, maybe it was longer – she came to me and without a word kissed me. It was the first time in months that we had kissed without being in a scene. It was warm, not demanding, not teasing or threatening. It was just a quiet, loving kiss and I was able to say to her, without a word, that I loved her, too.

So, we became a couple of a different kind after that. She no longer threatened to leave me, no longer caused me the pain of thinking we might separate; I no longer demanded fidelity and commitment from her but I think she gave me both. We no longer played Master-Slave but we did find a club in the city where for a short time on the week-ends we could be involved in bondage. Some of the old kick in that was still there, but mostly it was just fun stuff; and having other couples involved gave it a lot more excitement.

It's funny but when you've been through what we went through you think you know the other person but actually we only knew one small part of each other. What we began to see was that neither of us had ever really shared what we were about with anyone. We knew each other's bodies, probably better than most people know anyone's, but we didn't know anything about what went on inside each other's thoughts. We knew how to bring one another to the point of ecstasy or of terror but we didn't have a clue as to what made them who they were. What were their hopes and fears? We knew how much we valued being able to explore and express our passion but we didn't know squat about the other's values. We didn't even know whether we believed in a God, or in an after-life; or how we felt about kids; or what we wanted for our old age. We'd spent hours and hours paying attention to the smallest quivers in a muscle or in the color of the other's cheek but we didn't really know each other at all; and we weren't known by the other, either.

It must have been the fact that we had begun to trust one another's love that made it possible to begin to share all of these things. As we did there were large areas we agreed on and these made us feel good and drew us closer. And there were large areas we disagreed on – sometimes violently – and we would fight and scream and vow never to speak to one another again. But "never" usually meant until the next morning and then we'd get on with our lives. We sort of balanced getting closer and getting apart. The really great thing was that we had the juice flowing again. We felt alive. Marty felt alive and that was what really mattered. Without that, I think we would have drifted down to a place where she would have been miserable again.

We gave up a lot of our play, especially the kind that left marks or bruises. Every once in a while we would act out a scene – never pushing too far – so that we could get the rush that we used to get when we were punishing the other, or being punished. And through our club we were introduced to the "breathless O". Sometimes it resulted in O – orgasm, sometimes it didn't. But it had an element of danger in it that was just as exciting as some of the hitting and bondage. There was nothing fancy in it – a plastic bag over the head, taped shut around the neck - and a partner who agreed to tear it off at a pre-arranged signal. Usually you'd be having sex while this was going on and the orgasm was really intense – I mean it could be really, really intense – something about when there is no oxygen going to the brain your feelings are multiplied. Sometimes the person in the bag blacked out and then it got really scary getting the bag off and making sure they were breathing right. Sex didn't seem very good when this happened but most people kind of put these episodes behind them and went back to the routine over and over.

Marty and I played this out several times and we really looked forward to it. Then, we reasoned, if it was good for one person to be nearly suffocated when they climaxed, it could be better for both of us to use a bag and so we experimented with her bag being taped but my bag being really loose.

The experiment failed. My bag wasn't loose enough and I blacked out. Marty's hands were tied and she never woke up. I loved Marty.

The judge summed it up nicely, "an untimely and tragic end".

End of Scene 1

Scene 2

Setting: *Three months later.*

A prison cell – it could be the same as the one in Scene 1 – but with the addition of some touches to make it less austere and less like the death-row cell of Scene 1. (Calendars, posters, anything to add a bit of color.)

At rise the narrator is seated, leaning back and rocking slowly, with his feet up on the table.

So, that was, what? Two or three months ago? I made history. I'm the last person to have been sentenced to hang. Since then, there have been all sorts of variations put into use – lethal injection, gas, firing squad – and they're all the very favorite of some minority and are labeled inhumane or inefficient by others.

I had a simple, non-technical execution all set up and rarin' to go but isn't it just like a Grade B movie? Condemned man walks to the gallows, the warden offers the prisoner a hood (which I refused); the priest begins to pray – for the hangman and jury I guess – and the telephone rings. It rings and it rings and it rings and then suddenly, the fat-assed warden's eyes go as wide as saucers. I guess he realized who or what the call was and he actually falls down the steps of the gallows to get to the wall where the 'phone is. I can tell he hurt himself because there's tears streaming down his face even before he answers. He listens for a minute and then says, "thank-you" three or four times before he says "good night sir", "thank-you sir", "a pleasure talking to you sir". I mean, it's midnight, I'm standing there with a rope around my neck and he's driveling on like he's at a fricking social event.

He comes back to me, and tells me that I'll live to see the sunrise – my sentence has been commuted by the Governor. The priest took the noose off me and started blessing everyone around; then he turned to the spectators, waved a blessing on them and crossed himself maybe a dozen times as he walked me back to my cell.

So, here I am, still alive, death sentence commuted by a Governor who I guess actually took the trouble to read his letters. Like the letter from the blind guy from the trial who told me his name was Ted when he started visiting me a couple of days after my due date. Well, Ted told me he was there in court every day and that he took a keen interest in the proceedings and the outcome. It seemed to him that I might have gotten a very bum rap and that he was going to try to understand what really happened at the trial and how the jury decided I was guilty of murder.

My legal aid lawyer – can you believe it, a legal aid lawyer for a capital crime – argued that if I was guilty of anything it might be manslaughter or negligence causing death but that there was no evidence I had actually planned Marty's death. He did argue that there was no motive for me to kill Marty but the prosecutor tore into that on the grounds that a number of witnesses could be brought in who would testify that every once in a while I had become insanely jealous when Marty spent too much time or showed too much interest in other men – even if their connection was all part of the group scene we were involved in.

In the end he argued for the truth – that her death was accidental. But it was clear that the jury wasn't buying that approach. They had no doubts whatever and returned the murder verdict the same day they were given the case. In fact, the jury foreman, a guy I used to see around the plant whenever I went to pick Marty up said how much the jury appreciated how clear the prosecutor was in setting out the case against me. I don't know why it never occurred to anyone to ask whether this foreman knew Marty from work and whether they ever had a relationship of any sort, but no one asked. Fact is, when we were having one of our spats Marty used to talk about this guy and how she used to date him. Oh, well.

This old bird from the trial couldn't see the side of a barn until he walked into it but, man-oh-man he had a memory for things he heard; it was like he had a magnetic tape or a disc running between his ears from morning to night. Someone coughed while the judge was talking and he remember it and could tell you what was being said; someone in the jury rocked on their chair or wriggled he could tell you who it was. Uncanny!

When he first came to see me I didn't exactly know what he wanted so I wasn't overly friendly, sort of wary you might say. After a few minutes of bullshit he pulls his chair over to me, leans forward like he could actually see me eye-to-eye and tells me, "Now that I've saved your life, I aim to get you out of here."

What in hell! I figured this guy for a pan-handler or a trial junkie and now he's talking getting me off death row and out of the pen completely. Part of me wanted to have him thrown out, another part wanted to have him made a saint if he really did have something to do with keeping me alive, but the largest part was excited or maybe scared and I started to shake. He just put his hand out, laid in on the side of my head, sort of over my ear and said I'd be OK and he'd see me in a while, he had some research to do.

As I think back to that meeting I have to admit that as my new protector – or whatever he was – left my cell I could feel a hot tear sliding down my cheek. And what was that all about? I asked myself. Bum comes in claiming to be my Saviour and I don't ever want him to leave. What's that all about? I asked myself. I think I know now.

When Marty died I learned something about what makes a person a person. I figured I had a pretty good handle on who I was. I knew what I liked and didn't like, I knew what I was good at and where I'd been faking and I knew the kinds of people I liked to hang with. What I didn't have a clue about was that I depended on Marty to keep telling me who I was.

I'd wake up and if I grunted she'd either grunt back or try to humour me. If I was playful with her she might be playful back or maybe she'd want her own time and space. Every time she reacted to me it was like a kind of mirror. It didn't give me back a reflection of me, it gave back what I meant to her at that moment and that's the bottom line. Marty kept telling me who I was to her – what I meant to someone, someone I cared about.

So, when Marty went, she took that with her – my meaning, and I felt like I didn't exist anymore. She took a huge part of me with her – a part that no one else ever had and I don't think ever will. It's like she carried me around inside her – all her likes and dislikes about me – and when she went I didn't have anyone to reflect back to me, to show me who I was or what was good or rotten about me. Ted was the first person in a long time who seemed to think I mattered and I hated to see him go because I wasn't certain he'd ever come back.

After that, he pops by every now and then, says he's making progress. I asked him what in hell that meant and he talks about picking up the scent, or being out on the trap line. I truly believe he's crazy but visitors aren't exactly lined up to see me so I let him ramble on.

Ramble probably isn't exactly the word. He's putting together a story and on each visit there's another little bit that is somehow linked to earlier bits. Do you know what it's like dealing with someone who operates in his own world? These little bits I'm talking about are words that come with their own particular sounds – a hum or a snatch of melody, or a whistle. It's like he's got a whole library in his head and everything has its own sound. Trouble is, I don't know his filing system so it all seems like nonsense to me.

Last week something new happened. Ted comes in and stretches out his hand to shake mine. "Victim", he says (that's what he calls me), "when you get out of here you will owe me approximately $1000.00. That's calculating about $15 a night for beer and chips for two months of research." I don't know what in hell he's talking about until he explains that almost every night for two months he's been going to the local bars and coffee shops, telling waitresses and bartenders he's writing a story about me and my sickness. He's pretty well known to some of them and they open up to him and pretty soon he's introduced to one of the jurors from my trial. She talks and then she mentions another juror that she got to know and pretty soon Ted has spent time talking with several jurors about how sick and perverse Marty and me were. Of course Ted doesn't give two hoots about what they think – it's too late to argue they were biased at the trial – what he's looking for, actually who he's looking for, finally appears.

He meets up with a lady juror and the minute he hears her voice he says his head lit up like fireworks went off and for the last two weeks since he met her he's been, to use his words, "verifying the coordinates."

Now I still don't know squat but I'm happy Ted thinks he's on to something, or someone. Then I get a little curious about Ted, himself: who he is, where he came from, that sort of thing. "Victim", he says, "I'll tell you my life story next time I visit." And, sure enough, the next time I see him he's lugging this binder with three or four inch rings to it and he carefully feels his way to my table where he thumps it down.

One quick look at this collection of photos and newspaper clippings tells me first, someone else put this stuff together – it's far too neat for Ted to have done it, he's just not that organized; and second, he was at one time or another involved with the Courts – in some way.

"You're wondering, What does a blind man need with a scrap book? " asks Ted. "My daughter put it together after my accident. It's mostly for her and the grand- kids if they ever ask about me, but once in a while, like now, it's useful to haul it out."

I checked out a few pages and one of them, the front page of the local paper announced, "Prominent lawyer loses sight: remains conscious through rescue." There was a picture of a completely totaled car and beside it a tow-truck, an ambulance and a state trooper car. "Victim", says Ted, "that trooper car was the second one on the scene. There was one there before that one and it was being used as a cab to take the honorable local judge and a lady friend from a party to their homes. Everybody around the Courthouse heard about it. The press reported that the judge happened to be passing the site on state business but there was never a mention of any woman being present; but I heard her, I heard them laughing and her giggling while they waited for the tow truck. Once another trooper was on the scene they beat it."

"When I was in hospital the good judge came to visit me. Said he'd read about the accident and since he knew me from my appearances in front of him, he thought it would be good to drop by. He also had someone he called his wife with him. She didn't say much. Of course I couldn't see them but we all had a nice conversation about how God favors those who revere him and similar bullshit and they wished me well."

"Point of fact", says Ted, "I didn't do so well over the years but the honorable judge became Governor – the one that's still in the state capital."

By this point I'm ready to tell Ted to take his clippings and vanish but his story about the crash, the judge-who-is-now-Governor, and the lady who was riding with the judge has me a little intrigued.

"So, Victim, I spend some of my time watching my old colleagues ply their trade in Court and by the luck of the draw you got put in front of a really mean-assed, persuasive prosecutor that I used to date – back when he and I and our wives were real swingers. Oh yes, and the honorable judge, who wasn't Governor then, used to be right in the middle of it. Matter of fact, he took my ever-loving prosecutor away from me. I'd be lying if I said I ever forgave him.

"Anyways, when I read about you it seemed to me that with any sort of half-decent defense you wouldn't be found guilty of murder. Manslaughter maybe, maybe even a lesser charge. But, when I saw who the prosecutor was going to be I got really scared for you because I knew he had been on a crusade against what he calls "abominations" ever since he got religion and gave up his former hard drinkin', easy livin', freebasing sex.

"So, I got to thinking about how justice is sometimes more perverse than the so-called crimes which pass through the courts and I sent a friendly letter to the Governor reminding him of the good old days and that there was no statute of limitations on what the public would lap up from the tabloids. As far as I could tell, there might be a really good story about the night he wound up as one of the first cars on the scene of my accident and how it still might raise questions about why a state trooper and his car were being used to transport a local judge around the countryside; and whether or not said judge was alone or did he have female companionship; and whether said companionship was legally related to him or was it some other kind of relationship. And that, Victim, is how the Governor saw the light and was merciful upon thee."

So, this blind-as-bat derelict, former lawyer and swinger, engineered the commutation of my sentence. Yes, I owed him my life; but how did he propose to get me out of this cell and to be a free man again? That's what he had promised and at this point I wasn't prepared to doubt him.

Of course I had to ask him about the bar-hopping I'd apparently been paying for over the last two months, and about the woman's voice and the two weeks of "verifying the coordinates".

Ted explained things to me as though I was an eight-year-old. His story was basically this: he recognized the voice of one of the jurors as they made their way into and out of court and also during the jury selection process. He was positive it was the voice of the woman in the trooper's car and also the woman who accompanied the judge-who-became-the-Governor when he visited me. Once he met her in the bar he was absolutely certain.

For the two weeks after that he enlisted his daughter's help as a researcher and they scoured city records, tax rolls, old telephone books and even got some help from traffic court to check out old licenses. At the end of the two weeks Ted had an almost unbroken chain which stretched from the time the woman was selected as a juror in my case back to a time and place where she could easily have made contact with the Governor – then an honorable judge. Fact is, she made contact with half the police force and the lawyers in town but all Ted needed to know was that a case could be made for her having been with the Governor and that she was not his wife.

He admitted his first letter bordered on blackmail but thought he might present a second letter as being the results of historical documentation. He thought the Governor would be interested in what might be regarded as a chain of evidence. That would be the "verifying the coordinates" part of his work. The other part of the letter might deal with such matters as the prosecutor's former contacts with the Governor when they were both much younger. Then again, he might not include such information. He thought he might conclude the letter with the suggestion that a judicial review be ordered, or a mistrial be declared, and that while any or all of this was going on I should be released and after a few years of inaction on the part of the prosecutor's office a full pardon might be considered.

Marty and I lived as we wanted to. We loved, fought and connected in ways most of society found shameful or sick at best and as a violation of the natural order or God's will at worst. We gave pleasure to each other in ways that frequently hurt the body and sometimes struck the soul.

If I get to be a free man again I'll want to work for the falsely convicted and I want to spend a lot of time with Ted. I figure I can be his eyes - if he needs them.

Curtain

THE SHORTEST PLAY IN HISTORY

Note to the reader:

It's difficult to write what I want to about this play without giving away the punchline. Suffice to say, that when I first heard the story the participants, Sam and Al, along with their wives, were very close friends. They all had just returned, somewhat hung-over from a cottage week-end, and played out the story – perfectly naturally - in the middle of a coffee-break where we worked. Only later, much later, did we find out it had been a set-up.

Enough said, you'll see what I mean.

Cast of Characters

SAM: Any age and either male or female.

AL: Also any age and either male or female.

(The pronouns used in the script might need to be adjusted, depending on the intentions of the Director and Actors.)

SAM sits in an armchair leaning towards a laptop which is on a small coffee table in front of him. He alternates among writing, thinking, and chuckling - sometimes quietly, sometimes out loud.

AL is ensconced in a second armchair, trying to read, but clearly distracted by the actions and sounds from SAM.

AL

It's a good thing you're not writing a musical! You'd be dancing on the table-top. Can't you bottle it up!

SAM

My my, such intolerance for the arts. I'll have you know I'm engaged in one of the toughest intellectual facets of playwriting.

AL

Which is?

SAM

Getting beyond dialog and context; beyond setting and historical limitations; beyond mere existentialism.

AL

I haven't a clue what you're talking about. If you're beyond all that, what's left?

SAM

Essence, my friend, essence.

AL

Which is to say?

SAM

There are some plots and some situations which everyone will recognize instantly as being at the very heart of a situation - perhaps of their situation. I want to speak volumes without unnecessary words; reach the heart and mind of the audience in a true and honest way. In short, provide the essence or deeper meaning of what is spoken and shown on the stage.

AL

Gimmee a "for instance". What's the title of this mighty drama?

SAM

Believe it or not I've chosen to use humour - a joke - to explore an incredibly deep matter.

AL

That's why you've been pecking at it every week-end for what seems like months. Must be a hell of a long joke to require that much attention.

SAM

Not at all. In fact, in answer to your earlier question, the title is, "The Shortest Joke in History."

AL

Ah God, are you going to recycle some of those Knock-Knock jokes? I know one that's only four words long.

SAM

You do? How extraordinary! What is it?

AL

This is a joke about the 3rd World War. Knock, knock.

SAM

Who's there?

AL

(A long silence until he sees SAM looking quite
disgusted but actually suppressing a smile.)

Get it?

SAM

Yes, I get it. But the joke wouldn't work without the set-up. You have to tell your listener that it's in the context of a world war for it to make any sense. So the joke is actually a lot longer than two words and it demands that your audience actually knows how a 3rd World War would be fought.

Nice try, though.

AL

It's short and kinda philosophical, isn't it? So what's your joke? How long is it?

SAM

Well, it's a play in two acts and it's eight words long.

AL

Right. Two acts; eight words... and how many actors, pray tell?

SAM

Two.

AL

Wait! Wait! I just remembered Rodney Dangerfield's great four word gag. He used it in every performance. Of course he died before I could see him but I saw him on video and read about him. Somewhere in every monologue - so there was only one actor involved - he'd say, "Take my wife...please". Now that's cutting to the chase, I'd say. You don't need to know a hell of a lot more about him and his missus to know what he's saying there.

SAM

Granted. So maybe you win in terms of a monolgue but I think I have something along the same lines, only it involves two actors.

AL

No set-up?

SAM

Not only *no* set-up but the gag has a different meaning depending on what you know, or think you know about the actors and their relationships that aren't on stage.

AL

Too much, too much. Let's get on with it. Are you going to read the thing to me or not?

SAM

If you'd like. Of course I could go back to polishing the script.

AL

Polish, shmolish. Who's on stage. Let me hear it. Or is a pantomime. Oh, no. You said it had words. So...go! Lights up.

SAM

OK.

First Actor: How's your partner?
Second Actor: Better than yours.
       (beat)

AL

Hah! Hah! Very funny. Actually it is kinda funny. That's it?

SAM

That's it. That's Act 1.

AL

What do you mean, Act 1?

SAM

Well, the joke is a 2-act play and that's Act 1.

AL

You're serious, aren't you? OK, what's Act 2?

SAM

Act 2 comes after the tension has been heightened in Act 1 and it provides both the climax and the resolution.

AL

Come on now! *How's your partner?* We'll give you three words for that although it's really four. *Better than yours.* That's three. So you've used a whole six words up. Act 2 has eight words minus six equals the grand sum of two words for the whole act. And they are?

SAM

I know.

AL

OK, we agree, there are two words for the second act. What are they?

SAM

I know.

AL

What is this, some kind of echo chamber? And don't tell me you know, again.

SAM

That's Act 2. I know.

AL

I'm missing something here. Take it from the top, as you theater people like to say.

SAM

Sure. Actor 1 - How's your partner?
Actor 2 - Better than yours.
Actor 1 - I know.

AL

Umph! You know, that's really kind of a sick story. I don't think it's a joke at all. Two poor idiots discover that their partners have been in some kind of relationship with the person they're talking to. It boggles the mind.

SAM

It's a kind of Bob and Carol and Ted and Alice type of story. That was a classic film, wasn't it? Of course it could be a Mary and Joan and Sheila and Sally saga, too.

AL

Whaddya mean?

SAM

So, the first actor is Bob, who's married to Carol and Ted, who's married to Alice. Bob's making it with Alice and he finds out that the guy he's talking to is bedding Carol.

AL

Sick!

SAM

Used to happen all the time. Less so now, I think.

AL

Yeah. More likely now-a-days that Bob is married to Carol and she's making out with Alice, or that Carol is married to Alice. Then Bob finds this out from Ted who confesses his own relationship with Carol. It's something you would see on afternoon TV. Like I said, it boggles the mind.

SAM

Hey, my friend ... how's your wife?

Curtain